Reasons MARRIED

7 Secrets To Make The Right Decision

David Demaison

Order please contact: David Demaison, 25 The old stables, Ballinderry Lower, LISBURN, C. Antrim, BT28 2FY, United Kingdom

Interior Design by: Reality Premedia Services Pvt. Ltd.
First published in 2015 by David Demaison
Printed in Great Britain for Should i2 by:
Lightning Source UK Ltd
Chapter House, Pitfield Kiln Farm,
Milton Keynes
MK11 3LW
United Kingdom

Table of Contents

Introduction

As Herman H. Kieval correctly stated, "Marriage is a commitment – a decision to do, all through life, that which will express your love for one's spouse." Marriage is a beautiful relationship that must be built on love, trust, loyalty, respect and honesty. The absence of even one of these ingredients could create numerous problems, some of which could lead to a total breakdown.

This book was created with the purpose of helping readers to understand whether marriage would be the right decision to make. It aims to give you better insight into this institution, including the responsibilities, commitments and other factors that would be involved in making marriage your next step.

The first chapter begins by taking you on a journey through the history of marriage. You will find out how this commitment came into existence and the historical ceremonies and traditions of this union. The concept of marriage during ancient times and the reasons why people married during that period will also be discussed. The same chapter further explores how wedding rituals and marital obligations have changed in the modern world.

In the second section of the first chapter, you will find out about the various kinds of marriages. Every part of the world has different cultural and marital regulations and they will be discussed alongside the details of important laws.

The third part of the chapter will discuss relationships most commonly seen in the modern world. Times have changed; they have brought a dynamic change within the way that relationships are perceived and practiced. There are certain relationships that are unacceptable in some parts of the world, and even in different parts of the same country. These include cohabitation and homosexual relationships, both of which will be delved into deeper within this book.

In the fourth section, you will find out what roles religion does play in our modern world marriage. It also explores the different ceremonial practices observed when two people marry in a religious context. This will include marriages in Christianity, Judaism, Islam, Hinduism, Sikhism and Buddhism.

In the second chapter, you will learn about the various symbols of marriage in our society with also the regarded symbols that are associated with different religions including Judaism, Buddhism, Hinduism, Christianity and Islam.

The third Chapter of the book is highly interesting as it discusses a whole treasure of fascinating facts, superstitions and traditions about marriages in different places, cultures and religions. For example, did you know that if the bride finds a spider in her wedding gown on her wedding day, it would bring her good luck? (You might hear a scream before to experience the luck!)

In the fourth chapter, you will discover all the wrong reasons for getting married; it explains why one must never get married to a person for inappropriate or irrelevant reasons. One should always marry for the right reasons, some of which are also outlined in the third section.

The fifth chapter of the book is solely related to all the reasons that people consider when deciding to get married. There are many people who do not decide to marry someone because of love or attraction; many other reasons exist for people who decide to marry. These reasons include starting a family, having children, attachment needs, stability, financial and monetary benefits, and societal acceptance.

The sixth chapter gives you detailed insight into whether or not marriage is right for you. You will also become aware of all the concept and implication to expect when you may want to commit to someone. From the concept of commitment to balancing marriage and career, this chapter will help you to discover if marriage is something you desire.

This chapter is without doubt the highlight of the book. If you are doubtful about whether or not you should say "yes" to your partner's, then the seventh chapter is for you! It will help you to make that decision as smoothly as possible. It highlights seven important key questions that will lead you towards a solid decision about your marital opportunities and options.

The next chapter, number eight, takes a look at all the matter that are bound to change once you get married. Life after marriage could be significantly different to life with a partner before marriage. It simply could affect small things like your name, but also more important matter such as priorities as well as taking common decision has family.

Chapter nine sums up some of the pros and cons of getting married to help you in the actual decision-making process. In the tenth section, you will discover some beneficial resources and links related to online counselors, marital advice and marriage laws around the globe.

The last section concludes the book with a variety of tips that can help you apply all the information that you have gathered. The book aims to be highly useful for people considering marriage for the first time or perhaps second even third time, as well as those who are completely unsure about where they should even begin.

Chapter 1

About Marriage

Part 1: The History of Marriage

Marriage is a very old institution and its history dates back numerous centuries. There is no single confirmed date about its origin; the legends of marriage vary from culture to culture. Let's now look at the history of marriage, followed by the concept of this institution in ancient days and the reasons why people from that day and age wanted to marry. We will then proceed towards a review of how modern marriages have come into place.

History of Marriage

A man's wife has always been seen as a precious but dependent woman who remains in need of her husband's support. In ancient nomadic Middle Eastern communities and tribes, people used to practice *beena*, which is an ancient type of marriage.

In the context of *beena*, a wife had her own tent and was provided with complete liberty within the boundaries of that tent. Tribes living in parts of early Persia also observed this practice. Some passages extracted from the Bible also give examples of wives that had tents as their personal possessions. Sarah, Jael and the wives of Jacob are good examples of such wives.

The later parts of the Bible discusses that wives were provided with the innermost and most private rooms of her husband's abode. Those rooms were forbidden for men other than her husband. If a husband was wealthy, he would give the entire space of a house to his wife for her to enjoy her freedom. However, this life wasn't completely free; certain extracts from the Bible describe that every wife had to execute certain important household chores, which included sewing, spinning, weaving, cooking, bread-making, animal husbandry and fetching water. Back then, the Book of Proverbs contained a huge list of duties that a wife would have to perform.

There were also duties for the husband to carry out. According to the Covenant Code, if a man had two wives, then he had to make sure that he would not deprive his first spouse of the right to have food, clothing and sexual activities with him. If a husband failed to provide these things to her, the wife had the right to get divorced. According to the Talmud (central text of Rabbinic Judaism), it was compulsory for a husband to provide all his wives with food, clothing and sex.

Most of the tribes and communities living in ancient Persia practiced polygyny. According to this practice, a man could have more than one wife if he desired. Hence, there were no laws regarding marital fidelity in these communities. Nonetheless, according to prophet Malachi, a husband should not be unfaithful to his wife and should not divorce her as God does not like this act.

In ancient times, if a married woman committed adultery, she was charged with the death penalty. Similarly, if a man engaged in adultery with a married woman, he was also sentenced to death. The Priestly Code in the Book of Numbers states that if a woman carrying a child were suspected of being unfaithful to her husband, then she would be charged with the Ordeal of Bitter Water. In spite of all the punishments, adultery was practiced frequently by people of that era.

In the Ancient Greece, two people only needed to have a mutual consensus to get married; they only had to regard each other as wife and husband for their marriage to be accepted. No religious or civil ceremony was performed to unite them in wedlock. Normally, men married during their twenties and women in their teenage years. These ages were suitable because the Greek men completed their military service or became financially settled during their mid to late twenties, while young women could easily raise children if married early.

Married women were given certain rights in the ancient Greek community, but their main role was to manage the house and children. The Greek community believed that if someone married during the full moon, their marriage would be full of good fortune; in fact, most Greeks married during the winter season.

There were numerous kinds of marriages practiced in the ancient Roman communities. The conventional kind was known as *conventio in manum*. It comprised of a ceremony that was performed in the presence of witnesses. This type of marriage used to dissolve alongside a ceremonial practice. In this marriage, the wife lost all her rights of inheriting any asset from her family, but gained the same rights from her husband and new family. She was treated as her husband's authority.

Another kind of marriage was the *sine manu*. It was a free marriage and, in this kind, the wife had the right to stay as a part of her family. She used to keep the rights of inheriting assets from her father, but could not inherit anything from her husband. In the Roman tribes, girls as young as 12 were married like this.

In the early Germanic tribes and communities, both the groom and the bride were of a similar age when they entered matrimony. They also used to be older than the newlyweds of Roman tribes.

According to Aristotle, life's prime age was 37 and 18 years for men and women, respectively. This was the "right" age for both the genders to marry. However, as per the famous Visigiothic (Hispanic) Code of Law that was observed during the seventh century, the best age for men and women to marry was 20.

Early Concepts of Marriage and Reasons For Marriage

There were different concepts regarding marriage in the ancient tribes. Here are some of the most popular ones.

Strategic Coalition and Agreement

The Anglo-Saxons were amongst the earliest tribes of Britain. Their concept of marriage was that it was a strategic agreement between two people. Marriage was viewed as a tool that helped in establishing trade and diplomatic ties. Stephanie Coontz, the author of the famous book *Marriage, A History: How Love Conquered Marriage*, writes: "You established peaceful relationships, trading relationships, mutual obligations with others by marrying them."

The major reason why people of that tribe married was also to form strategic relationships with and gain benefits from prospective clients. Parents took special care in marrying their children to someone and would consider the person's financial condition and net worth before allowing any marriage to take place.

Bride's Consent Was Trivial

When a woman was married in the 11th century, her parents rarely asked for her consent. Numerous times, the groom was also left unasked about whether or not he was ready to marry a certain girl; he was tied into matrimony for the sake of gaining a political or economic advantage from the bride's family.

Things changed to some extent when Gratian, a Benedictine monk, asked people for their consent when they married someone during 1140. He specified the rules pertinent to marriage in *DecretumGratiani*, his textbook on law. According to this book, couples entering matrimony must express their consent verbally and must consummate their marriage to seal the bond. The marriage policies of the Church were formed according to the laws presented in the book during the 12th century.

Marriage – A Sacrament

During the early twelfth century, Roman Catholic writers and theologians referred to matrimony as reparation. It was a sacrament that enabled people to experience the presence of God. During 1563, the Council of Trent gave marriage the official status of a sacrament. Hence, some people of the Catholic communities did marry to understand the presence of God and feel it near them.

However, marriage did not have the same status according to the Protestant theology, which is why the Council decided to clarify the place of marriage in the society. Elizabeth Davies of the Catholic Bishops' Conference of Wales and England stated that some people assumed marriage to be a sacrament, but this was clarified to be false during 1563.

Wedding Vows

The wedding vows originate from the time of Thomas Cranmer. He was an architect belonging to English Protestantism. He scripted the concept of marriage vows about 500 years back in a text titled *Book of Common Prayer*.

Almost everything that people say during their wedding vows, such as "for better or for worse" and "from this day forward", originated from that book.

Civil Marriages

France was, after the 1789 revolution, the first country to declare in 1792 religious marriage ceremonies secondary. Religious ceremonies could only be proceed after previously been registered and married during a civil ceremony. Napoleon spread the tradition across Europe during his many campaigns. Today the civil union in France is still the only legal marriage. Often after, religious ceremonies take place but will not have any legal recognition.

According to the Marriage Act in 1863, people of a different religion were allowed to hold their civil marriages in the offices of the registrars in Old Britain. These offices were established in various cities and towns across Wales and England. The Catholic couples and nonconformists were also allowed to marry in their holy venues of worship.

The state also began maintaining statistics and records of marriages.

The Entry of Divorce

Divorce wasn't a very acceptable or common concept in ancient times. Prior to 1858, there were hardly any married people who divorced their spouses. During 1670, the English Parliament finally passed a rule that allowed John Manners, Lord Roos, to officially divorce his wife, Lady Anne Pierpon. This event acted as a model for parliamentary acts pertaining to divorce. In Manners' case, the divorce took place due to the adulterous behavior of his wife.

This episode gave birth to modern divorce. From the late 17th century until the mid-19th century, there were only over 300 divorce cases but each of those cases required an act by the Parliament. Eventually, in 1858, it was allowed for divorce to be carried out via a legal process. Nonetheless, divorce was still an unaffordable option for many people as the lawsuits and legal processes were expensive back then. In addition to this, wives engaging in adultery or charged of such a crime had to prove that their respective spouses were guilty of desertion, incest, cruelty, bigamy, bestiality or sodomy, according to Rebecca Probert of the University Of Warwick School Of Law.

The Divorce Reform Act initiated in 1969 opened the pathway for divorce. Couples were no longer required to state the exact reason of the divorce; they could just state that their marriage wasn't working as expected.

Bren Neale, a sociologist from the University of Leeds, stated that marriage was seen as an everlasting institution before 1969. However, the divorce law changed things. It allowed people living a terrible marriage to escape and live a better life. Marriage was no longer viewed as an ultimate commitment; rather, the concept was changed to a personal commitment that required individuals to feel fulfilled and happy.

State Control

In 1753, the state also became more involved in marriage due to the Lord Hardwicke's Act, also referred to as the Clandestine Marriage Act 1753.

According to this act, a couple wanting to marry each other had to do so in a chapel or church and their service had to be performed by a certified minister. If these conditions were not met, their union was considered as void. Couples were also required to officially announce their marriage or acquire a marriage license.

The majority of the newlyweds were abiding by these rules as they were mentioned in the Cannon Law, but this act also created penalties that they had to go through if they did not comply with the act. These penalties were much harsher than before. Non-marital relationships between people were not particularly respected by the state.

A Comparison of Marriage in the Ancient and Modern Times

There is a huge difference in the concept of marriage as it was previously viewed and as it is seen now.

In ancient years, marriage was a lifelong commitment that could not be broken and has to be fulfilled for as long as the couple lived. Even if one of the spouses was suffering in the relationship, it could not be terminated. However, the changing times provoked a revolution. Slowly, people began accepting the idea of divorce and were allowed to end their marital life if their spouse was unkind or unfaithful. However, there had to be a judicious reason with proof for the English Parliament to sanction a couple's divorce.

With the passage of time, couples weren't always required to present a reason and its evidence, and could soon split up on the basis that their marriage just wasn't working well.

Another aspect that changed in marriage during modern times was the status of the wife. In ancient times, a wife had numerous responsibilities that she had to fulfill in order to please her husband. However, in modern times, it is obviously no longer compulsory for a wife to execute all the household chores, with **generally** the husband taking fully part in the household duties.

In the old days, procreation was amongst the major reasons of marriage. If someone wanted to have children and a family, they had to marry someone. This concept also changed during the late 19th century. As medical and health services improved and progressed, more children began surviving; this resulted in a huge increase in the average size of families. This led the married couples to lean towards contraceptive measures to prevent their family from becoming extra-large.

The idea of doing something to avoid having a child was forbidden during the early 17th and 18th century; people did not even discuss such an option. However, this has changed in the modern world and people are now strongly encouraged to use birth control options if they are not ready for children.

Furthermore, unmarried couples are commonly seen having children nowadays. This scenario was completely inconceivable a few centuries ago. In case, it did happen, the consequences would be severe especially for the mother. She would be forced to leave the house, her family and would be denied of inheritance. She wouldn't have any chance to get married either. Often the child born from unknown father would have very limited chance in life, especially if the mother was at young age. The child would also be treated poorly by the society and was labeled as a 'bastard' and 'illegitimate child.'

Another concept that has evolved in the modern world is cohabitation. A person was previously not allowed to stay with another person of the opposite gender if they were unmarried. However, cohabiting couples are now seen frequently. This concept began gaining popularity during the late 20th and early 21st century. Still, there are numerous countries where this concept is still disliked by society, but it is very common in the western countries.

Marrying someone of the same gender was a whole new issue – not only was it socially unacceptable, but it was not even considered to be a legal marriage. Same-sex couples were viewed as an abomination and were treated with what bordered on hatred. During the start of the 21st century, this concept began gaining ground and more people opened up to it. Nowadays, homosexual couples are provided with similar rights and privileges heterosexual in many parts of the world, most specifically in western countries.

How Has Marriage Evolved From the Past to the Present?

Marriage has undergone much evolution from the ancient times to the present day. In the past, a married couple did not need any understanding or compatibility in order to get married. If the families of the two individuals had decided it was time for them to get married, then little could change their decision. Two individuals were married without any knowledge about each other's past or present. People who married according to the consent of their parents were also given more respect by the society around them.

This scenario has now completely changed. It is not considered wise for a person to marry someone just because their elders asked them to do so; people now want to know each other before getting married. This information helps them to select the right partner: someone who they can spend a comfortable life with. Also, people who take time to marry or those who marry according to their own wishes are no longer disrespected by the wider society.

This behavior is mostly observed in western countries where people are allowed to practice what is known as a love marriage. However, it is now emerging speedily in many Asian and South Asian countries. There is still a considerable amount of population in these regions that considers love marriage as a big taboo; this trend is still prevalent in the rural areas of these regions, but the urban areas have modernized and now give sufficient rights to individuals and their marital decisions.

Another interesting trend is regarding the expectations of spouses from one another when they get married. Earlier on, a person who wanted to marry expected their spouse to love them, care for them and respect them. Husbands expected their wives to execute all the household chores and leave the job of earning their livelihood to them alone. The husband was considered the breadwinner of the family and had the sole responsibility of providing food, clothes and shelter for his family.

This concept also has changed vastly, mainly in the west. It is not compulsory for the husband to earn for the family; his wives now contribute to the family income as well. Both spouses share equal responsibilities in managing their house, finances and other social responsibilities. In the past, it was the main duty of the wife to take care of the children. The husband would hardly play any role in raising his children. This attitude and behavior has now changed: both spouses divide duties when it comes to taking care of their children and nurturing them.

Another change that can be widely seen today is regarding people's perception of marriage. Earlier on, marriage was seen as a solution to all problems – it was a means to have stable life and a family. If someone suffered from a disease, incredibly as it sounds, the religious priests would advise the person to get married in order to cure their ailment. This behavior is now completely obsolete.

People do not marry each other to put an end to their troubles. Rather, they marry to be closer to one another and to experience life together. Of course, there are still some cases in which people don't marry for love, but to enjoy certain benefits, or to attain a better financial state, privilege and other benefits. Nonetheless, most modern marriages fortunately take place because of mutual love and respect, despite any other issues they could or will face and this is what is most important.

Part 2: The Types and Laws of Marriage

Marriage has evolved over time and different kinds of marriages now exist, some of which are actually forbidden in certain religions and countries.

Monogamy

This is a commonly practiced type of marriage. In monogamy, an individual only has one spouse in the entire course of his or her life at one time. If the spouse dies, then the individual may or may not remarry – this depends on their beliefs, needs and attachment to the deceased spouse.

Monogamy is practiced almost everywhere in the world, including the Indian subcontinent, Europe, America and several parts of Asia. Countries that do not allow polygamy consider the marriage of a married person with another individual as bigamy, thus labeling it as a crime.

Divorce is not a difficult concept in countries where monogamy is exercised. Remarriage and divorce gives birth to serial monogamy. It means that a person had several marriages, but had only one spouse at one time.

Plural or Group Marriage

Plural or group marriage is a branch of polyamory and is also referred to as a "multi-lateral marriage". In this type of marriage, three or more people create a family and all the other members in that group are married to one another. If they have children, then all the members will share responsibilities related to the children's lives.

In the past, it was practiced by different tribes in Asia, Polynesia, Americas and Papua New Guinea.

Child Marriage

If a child younger than 18 is married to an adult or to another child, the marriage is termed as child marriage. It was commonly practiced in ancient times, but modern education, increased awareness and human rights organizations have improved things.

Child marriages were basically performed to secure the future of the children, to provide a family for the female child in the long run, and as a means of saving the family's inheritance. In most of the cases of child marriages, a young girl is married to an older man. It is mostly practiced in the Indian subcontinent, sub-Saharan Africa and South Asian countries like Afghanistan, Nepal, Iran, Sri Lanka, Maldives and Bhutan. However, it is not practiced by the educated class in these countries and is strongly frowned upon in western countries.

Child marriage results in numerous problems, including domestic violence, miscarriages, early births and even fatalities.

Third Gender and Same-Sex Marriages

Same-sex marriages are quite common in western countries. In a same-gender marriage, two individuals of the same sex get married. These marriages are also referred to as gay and lesbian marriages if the two individuals are either males or females, respectively.

Another concept that is closely related to same-sex marriage is third-gender marriage. In this marriage, a transgender person marries somebody of the same or opposite gender to which they have changed.

There are 17 countries in the world including Argentina, Belgium, Brazil, Canada, Denmark, France, Iceland, Luxembourg, the Netherlands, New Zealand, Norway, Portugal, South Africa, Spain, Sweden, the United Kingdom, and Uruguay plus certain sub-national jurisdictions (parts of Mexico and most states of the United States), that now allow same-sex union.

There has been a constant debate throughout the whole of Europe on the issue of same-sex marriage but there is no country in Europe who has a law against homosexuality. Belgium, Denmark, France, Iceland, Luxembourg, Netherlands, Norway, Portugal, Spain, Sweden, the United Kingdom are the countries in Europe where marriages is legal.

In United-States thirty-six out of the fifty states have legal sex marriage.

The establishments of Bulgaria, Hungary, Belarus, Latvia, Moldova, Lithuania, Poland, Slovakia, Ukraine and Serbia prohibit same-sex marriages.

Other countries where same sex marriages are banned are Angola, Algeria, Botswana, Cameroon, Burundi, Egypt, Comoros, Eritrea, Gambia, Ethiopia, Ghana, Kenya, Guinea, Lesotho, Liberia, Malawi, Libya, Namibia, Senegal, Nigeria, Seychelles, Somalia, Sudan, Tanzania, Swaziland, Tunisia, Togo, Zimbabwe, Uganda, Afghanistan, Bhutan, Bangladesh, India, Brunei, Pakistan, Kuwait, Iran, Malaysia, Lebanon, Myanmar, Maldives, Oman, Saudi Arabia, Syria, United Arab Emirates, Yemen, Uzbekistan, Qatar, Palestine, Singapore, Barbados, Antigua & Barbuda, Dominica, Belize, Grenada, Jamaica, Guyana, St Lucia, St Kitts & Nevis, Trinidad & Tobago, St Vincent & the Grenadines, Cook Islands, Indonesia, Nauru, Kiribati, Samoa, Tonga, Tuvalu and Solomon Islands.

Temporary Marriages

Temporary marriages are not permanent relationships and are practiced in various cultures. The handfasting marriage (is a component of a wedding ceremony which entails gently wrapping cords around the bride and groom's clasped hands and tying a knot, symbolically binding the couple together in their declaration of unity) is an apt example of temporary marriage. The fixed-term contractual marriage practiced in the Arab countries is also a common example.

Endogamy and Exogamy

Cultures that practice endogamy do not marry their children to individuals who do not belong to their specific class, race, and religion or ethnic group. For instance, in India, a person belonging to the Kshatriya class is not allowed to marry a person belonging to a lower class, such as Shudra class.

The opposite of endogamy is exogamy. In exogamy, a marriage between two individuals can only take outside their social groups.

Taboo Marriages

There are certain marital relationships that are deemed taboo in the modern world. They were practiced during ancient times, but the governments of most of the countries across the globe do not consider them legal anymore.

Marriages taking place between children and parents, between siblings, or between children and close relatives – such as maternal or paternal aunts and uncles – are forbidden in most part of the world.

Avunculate marriages are a good example of taboo or incest marriages. These marriages take place between a nephew and his aunt or a niece and her uncle. They are illegal in most countries, except Australia, Malaysia, Austria, Russia and Argentina.

Laws Related to Marriage

There are certain laws related to marriage. These laws are the legal demands and requirements that must be fulfilled. These laws include giving both the spouses control over their sexual services, property and labor. The spouses are given the responsibility of each other's debts and the right to visit the other when they are hospitalized. Additionally, they are given control over one another's affairs when one is incapacitated, establishing the legal guardian of their child, setting up a joint account or fund for the children's benefit, and establishing a healthy relationship amongst the members of the spouse's families.

These responsibilities vary from society to society, and religion to religion as well.

Children Strengthen the Marital Bond

This isn't a law, but a large number of people entering a marital relationship consider it important to have children. Children are considered to strengthen their bond and make it unique. There is a certain population that believes that having children is the only way to create a bond between the married couple.

This trend was particularly common in the ancient days when married couples were forced to have kids as soon as they got married. If a couple did not have children during their first year of marriage, the wife would be insulted, ridiculed and had to experience severe atrocities committed by her husband and in- laws. In some cases, she was even divorced and shamed by her community.

This trend has now greatly changed. If a couple does not have children in our modern world it could simply be because they have made a choice to not to. In infertility cases, the couple can resort to other means like surrogacy, IVF and artificial insemination. It is interesting to note that many married couples still consider it important to have babies.

Part 3: Relationships of the Modern World

The relationships existing between two individuals have undergone drastic modifications in recent times. The relationships that were once considered taboo in ancient times are now conveniently and comfortably practiced by more recent generations.

Listed below are some relationships that are commonly seen in the modern world.

Cohabitation

Cohabitation is a commonly practiced and popular relationship of the modern world. It is a special arrangement in which two people decide to live together. It can usually start as a short-term relationship, which becomes a long-term relationship, with families and children's involved, but it is not considered as an official or legalized marriage.

The individuals who practice cohabitation mainly agree on this arrangement, as they do not want to marry each other too soon, or sometimes at all. A cohabiting couple may or may not share different kinds of responsibilities with each other. For instance, if a cohabiting couple wants, they can share the financial and social responsibilities like married couples do.

Cohabitation was started in the Scandinavian areas and countries. Mediterranean Europe wasn't open to this relationship at first, but during the mid-1990s, a rise in cohabitation was observed in this region. Countries where Hinduism and Islamic Law are practiced do not accept this relationship and look down upon it. Saudi Arabia, Nepal, Bhutan, Iran, Afghanistan and Bangladesh do not accept cohabitation.

There are several reasons that have given birth to a rise in cohabitation. One reason is the empowerment of women. In ancient times, a woman was considered as being under a man's authority and it was compulsory for a woman to get married so that she could live a happy life. An unmarried woman did not enjoy a respectful status and legal rights like a married woman did. In fact, women were entirely dependent on their husbands for their survival.

Fortunately, this scenario has drastically changed in recent times. Women have been provided with better and increased rights that have strengthened them and made them completely independent from their male counterparts.

Another reason and probably the main one behind this shift is that people do not find marriage an obligation anymore. Marriage is not considered to be the right relationship for everyone. If a person does not feel comfortable in getting engaged and married to someone, perhaps wants to live a free life where they are not bound to another person, then they can practice cohabitation.

Some people also get involved in cohabitation if they have a fear of everlasting commitment. People who have witnessed marital problems between their parents during their childhood normally experience this type of fear. This fear prevents them from indulging in an ultimate relationship with any individual.

There is a certain population that practices cohabitation, as they do not want to be tied down with responsibilities and commitments pertaining to one person their entire life. They feel that marriage will ruin the love they have for their partner and will produce complex problems in the long run.

Same-Sex Union and Marriage

Another modern relationship is a same-sex union. In this relationship, individuals of the same gender decide to live together or get married. It is also referred to as a gay marriage or relationship, and a lesbian relationship if the two individuals in the relationship are women.

Same-sex marriages were condemned in a major part of the world but, gradually, people are now becoming more open to such relationships. As stated in the previous chapter, most countries do not allow this relationship and have prohibited it in their legal system.

In the past, western countries in Oceania, Antarctica, America and Europe frowned upon gay marriage. However, the various human rights organizations started recognizing their rights and began giving them a legal status. Movements for gay liberation initiated during the end of the 1960s motivated homosexuals to publicly "come out" and accept their sexual orientation. These movements are also often labeled as LGBT movements, which is an acronym for Lesbian, Gay, Bisexual and Transgender. These movements have helped people to live a better life and be accepted not only socially, but also into their own families. In 2011, a National Survey from the *William Institute* found that approximately 3.5% of the American population was identified as LGBT, which represents around 9 Million people.

As of 1 January 2015, there are 17 countries including Argentina, Belgium, Brazil, Canada, Denmark, France, Iceland, Luxembourg, the Netherlands, New Zealand, Norway, Portugal, South Africa, Spain, Sweden, the United Kingdom, and Uruguay plus certain sub-national jurisdictions (parts of Mexico and most states of the United States), that now allow same-sex union.

Bisexual relationship

A bisexual relationship involves a person that is attracted to both genders – both men and women.

According to the same previous US National survey from the *William Institute* in 2011, from the 3.5% of adult in America recognizing themselves as LGBT's 1.8% of them consider been bisexual. It also mention women significantly are more likely to identify as bisexual rather than men.

Another report released in 2007 during showed that 14.4 percent of the young women considered themselves as not completely heterosexual and 5.6 percent of young men in the U.S. considered themselves as bisexual or homosexual.

Bisexuality was also frequently practiced in ancient civilization like the Roman society or antique Greece. Similar relationships in the past were also observed in feudal Japan, Persia and South Pacific.

However, things have changed in modern times. A few countries now give equal rights to bisexuals and LGBT. These include Burkina Faso, Benin, Cote d'Ivoire, Cape Verde, Niger, Sierra Leone, Chad, Central African Republic, Democratic Republic of the Congo, Gabon, Equatorial Guinea, Rwanda, Madagascar, Mayotte, Lesotho, South Africa, Canada, Greenland, Bermuda, Mexico, Costa Rica, El Salvador, Guatemala, Panama, Nicaragua, Honduras, Aruba, British Virgin Islands, Cayman Islands, Cuba, and the majority of states in America.

All the countries where bisexuals and LGBTs are recognized provide these individuals with the following rights:

- Right to donate their blood

- Right to adopt children

- Recognition of their status by the government

- Anti-bullying

- Equality in immigration laws

- No discrimination

- Equality in age of consent laws

- Access to reproductive technology and sex reassignment surgery

- Legal recognition

- Rights to participate in military

Open Relationships

An open relationship is one in which the two participating individuals can have several sexual, emotional or romantic partners at the same time. This relationship is prohibited in the countries governed by Hinduism, Islam, Buddhism and Judaism.

Trends Observed in Modern Relationships

There are certain trends observed in modern relationships that are different to those that existed in the past.

- **Right Time:** Whether an individual is heterosexual or homosexual or bisexual, they tend to wait for the right time to arrive in their life before settling down with one person. Whether because of their career or their financial situation, either they want to get married or live as a cohabiting couple, they always wait for the most appropriate moment in their life before making this important decision. In the past, people used to settle down or marry an individual on reaching a certain age. For instance, our grandparents did not wait to set up their career or "enjoy life" before getting married, simply because the concept of the right time wasn't common during those days. It was more a matter of age, tradition and social pressure; even expectation that came from close friends or family.

- **Right Person:** It is quite common for someone to wait for Mr. or Mrs. Perfect (at least a look-like) to come along before tying the knot with someone. Not that long ago, the chance to find the right person was a lot more limited as people did not travel as much or did not have the actual possibility to reach internet to find their compatibility, and yet were managing to live happy marriages.

- **Get More Experience:** Couples wanting to get married are asked to get more experience and know about themselves and each other completely before entering into wedlock. This wasn't the case in the past when one was hurried into marriage as soon as they entered their 20s, or even their teenage years. Modern couples often wait for years to propose to each other or to cohabitate. This behavior seems to be more common in the urban areas.

- **Stay Single for Longer:** It is common for a person to stay single for a longer period than in the past. Our grandparents were happily married in their early 20s – or sometimes even earlier – while, nowadays, depending on where you are coming from, 25 years old could be considered as a young age to settle down with a person. If a person in their mid-20s wants to get married, they are often advised by their elders to wait for some more time and pay more thought to the decision.

- **Seek Love:** One of the major reasons why people wait more before getting married is that they seek love. Of course, people marry when they fall in love. If a person doesn't fall in love with someone, it is most likely that they won't marry which seems normal and obvious nowadays, but a lot less 100 or even 50 years ago. At that time, if you were seen with someone, it was perceived as a life commitment, especially if your relatives were introduced to that person. Even now in some cultures, if parents or relatives of an individual arrange their marriage, they still prefer knowing their spouse-to-be a little before tying the knot with them. This wasn't common in the past as the reasons to get married were simply an arrangement between two families. Individuals in the open world as we live, obviously dislike being pushed around, particularly into marriage arranged by relatives. The times have brought enormous changes, but still some cultures manage to keep those traditions alive.

- **Fear of Marriage:** It simply could be from the fear of commitment, but is also often expressed by an adult child of divorce (A.C.O.D.). They have this unconscious feel that their marriage may end up in divorce, just like their parents. The memories of fights and uncomfortable marital life lived by their parents result in the children resenting the idea of a lifelong commitment. In fact The National Opinion Research Council of America released a survey in 1999 demonstrating that Adult Children of Divorce are 50% more likely to divorce compared to an intact home.

Important Notes: It should be noted, that geo-localization especially in our modern world could have a serious impact on your behavior regarding marriage. For instance, an American survey of only five-year data proves that there are regionals inconsistencies in the average age of marriage predominantly supported by the individual location. The difference is mainly due to lifestyle, population density and most importantly the all attitude regarding personal life expectation. For example a relatively low populated state like Utah (say "rural") would see on average a women getting married at 23.5 years old and men 25.6 years old, whereas New york State (say "urban") would see the average marriage age for women at 28.8 years old and 30.3 years old for men. The highest would be Washington D.C with an average of respectively 29.8 and 30.6 years old for women and men, that makes more than 6 years differences between Utah and Washington D.C. Relatively impressive differences looking as a whole nation, certainly with some similarity observed with other developed countries around the world, leading us to conclude the more urban is the lifestyle, the later we tend to get married.

Part 4: Marriage and Religion

Marriage and religion have always been associated for centuries. Meanwhile time and society has also changed people regarding their personal belief and also their relation toward religion. Nonetheless, religion is still an important part of marriage in our modern society.

What Role Does Religion Play in Marriage in the Modern World?

It is quite normal for two individuals to fall in love not knowing whether they share the same believes. After all, love does not have boundaries and it cannot stop you to fall in love with someone from a completely opposite religion and faith. In the old days, it was never easy to travel, meet new people from different countries, cultures, and traditions. However, this trend is commonly observed nowadays, especially from the young generation. Students studying in universities across the world or sometimes people visiting Europe, the Americas or Oceania in search for a better living meet people from different religions and fall in love.

Nowadays, people do value their spiritual beliefs, nonetheless discovering new countries and population having different aspiration than them is considered a good idea as it will eventually broaden their mind, not only on the basic society concepts of living, but also more importantly spiritually. Of course people value their faith and hold it to great importance, but they may still fall for a person belonging to another religion. In such cases, it is crucial for those two people to consider their religious values as much as the beliefs of their partner. In most cases, the two individuals do marry and live a comfortable life together carrying their own personal beliefs.

Sometimes religion does not create havoc in their lives until they have children of their own. Raising children according to one's own religion is what makes life difficult for the two people. Both would like their own religion to have a strong influence on their kids. This issue often creates a rift between the two.

However, such awkward scenario does not always take place. There are numerous interfaith marriages across the globe that have survived these obstacles and have emerged as very successful.

An article published in *The Economist* on 13th April 2013, stated that a study conducted in the U.S. revealed that almost 45 percent of all the marriages that took place in the past ten years involved people from different faiths. This trend is mostly observed in the Americans, followed by the Jewish population.

In most cases of interfaith marriages, it has been observed that the families of the two individuals desiring to get married were against this idea. They did not feel comfortable if their children marry someone from an entirely opposite religion and culture, and go against the laws of their faith. Nonetheless, the two beings in love do marry each other and consummate their love with marriage. To them, a religious difference does not really matter in this scenario and they have the capacity to live a convenient life without meddling into the religious affairs of one another.

One must also look at the atheist's concept of marriage while discussing this subject. Atheists do not believe in God, but they do believe in the institution of marriage. According to the atheists, religion should not at all govern marriage and a person must be allowed to marry anyone they want. Marriage must be judged according to the merits and demerits of this institution, and not according to what religion one practices.

Numerous atheists have married other atheists as well as individuals of other faiths, and they are living a happy marital life. This is possible when the two married beings do not interfere in each other's religious matters. Atheist spouses do not like being dragged to religious ceremonies, nor do they want to be lectured on accepting the presence of God. As long as their wishes are fulfilled, they will happily support their spouse.

Another interesting fact about atheist marriages is that their divorce rate is much lower compared to that of Christian marriages, as illustrated by a study conducted in 2008. A representative from the survey also pointed out the atheists and agnostics have lower rates of marriage and a higher likelihood of cohabitation. As atheists do not believe in any religion, they aren't forced by any law to marry at a certain time or due to specific condition; they can enter into matrimony whenever they please.

What are the main marriage ceremonies in different religions?

A marriage ceremony depends on many different factors. Take a look below at how marriage takes place in the major religions.

Christianity

Marriages in Christianity are based on the teachings of Jesus Christ and Apostle Paul. Numerous denominations consider marriage as sacrament and Christians normally marry due to religious reasons. However, these reasons have changed with time.

Divorcing the spouse and remarrying was not at all encouraged in the past, but these aspects have also seen considerable development in modern society. The laws related to Christian marriages include honoring your marriage to someone and the non-obligation for everyone to get married. However, according to the New Testament, a person must only indulge in sexual activities with their spouse. Having sexual relationships with a person outside of marriage is adultery and a crime, according to Bible.

The ceremonies in a Christian wedding include the following:

- **Prelude:** Music is played in the place where the ceremony is supposed to take place.

- **Processional:** The bridesmaids walk up the aisle, followed by the bride with her father. The groom and his best men's are already waiting for them at the marriage alter.

- **Minister Introductions:** The minister greets everyone and introduces the bride and groom. They then perform a prayer for the soon-to-be-married couple.

- **Exchange of Vows:** The bride and groom exchange their marriage vows.

- **Exchange of Wedding Rings:** The bride and groom exchange their wedding rings.

- **Pronouncement of Matrimony:** The minister pronounces the couple as husband and wife.

- **First Kiss:** The minister introduces the couple as husband and wife and asks the groom to kiss the bride in order to seal their bond.

- **Lighting a Unity Candle:** In some Christian weddings, the bride and groom light a unity candle to bring them good luck.

- **Present-Giving Ceremony:** In some weddings, the bride and groom give presents to their respective mothers. This is an optional event.

- **Closing Prayer:** The minister closes the ceremony with a prayer.

- **Recessional:** Music is played and the bride and groom go outside, followed by their guests.

- **Party:** There is usually a party or reception after the ceremony where the bride and groom cut their wedding cake and the bride throws her bouquet towards her bridesmaids. It is said that the woman who catches the bouquet will be next to get married.

There are numerous symbols in Christian marriages, including the wedding cake, wedding gown, unity candles, wedding rings, boutonniere, rice throwing, and the bride carrying something old, new, borrowed and blue. These symbols will be looked at later in more detail.

Judaism

Jewish marriages are carried out according to the laws and regulations described in the Torah. According to Torah law, marriage is a two-step process. The first stage is called "*Kiddushin*," and the second step is known as "*Nisu'in.*"

By Talmudic times, a betrothal celebration followed the signing of the *Ketubah* (marriage contract). The groom gave the bride an object valued at less than a *Prutah* (small coin) and declared in the presence of two witnesses: "Be thou consecrated to me, be thou betrothed to me, be thou my wife." The actual wedding, approximately a year later, was preceded by a lively procession escorting the bride to the home of the groom.

Today, the betrothal and wedding generally both take place under the *Chuppah* (wedding canopy). As is still the custom today in traditional communities, the celebration continued for seven days at festive meals where the *shevaberakhot* (abundant blessing) were repeated following the grace after meals. Also important a Jewish married couple is also expected to procreate rapidly after marriage.

The ceremonies in a Jewish wedding are:

- **KabbalatPanim:** The bride and groom must not see one another for about seven days before the wedding day. They also greet their guests separately, which is referred to as *kabbalatpanim.*

- **Badeken:** The bride wears a veil and enters the wedding venue.

- **Chuppah:** The ceremony is organized beneath a *Chuppah*, which is a canopy. It symbolizes the new home the bride and groom will live in.

- **Blessings of Kiddushin:** The rabbi blesses the couple over a cup of wine and the bride and groom drink from that cup.

- **Exchange of Wedding Bands:** The groom then gives a ring to the bride, and the bride can also give him a ring if she wants to.

- **Ketubah:** This is the marriage contract and it outlines the responsibilities of both the spouses towards one another.

- **Seven Blessings:** Seven blessings, also known as *shevaberakhot*, are recited by the rabbi over another glass of wine.

- **Glass Breaking:** The couple breaks the wine glass as a sign of good luck to their marriage years.

- **Yichud:** The married couple is taken to a room and left alone for a little while.

- **Seudah:** This is the festive meal that all the guests enjoy eating after the ceremony has concluded.

Islam

In Islam, Muslims are commanded to get married by their holy book, the Quran. Islam allows polygyny, but not polyandry. The age of marriage is not defined, although the importance of the partner having gone through puberty is specified.

In a Muslim wedding, the bride, groom and bride's guardian must agree to the relationship. If the guardian disagrees, the marriage does not usually take place, as per certain cultures. The minimum demands the groom has to fulfill include providing housing, food, clothing and sexual satisfaction to his bride. For a marriage to be made official there should be two witnesses from the side of the bride and groom. The husband and wife both have the right to a divorce. However, there are strict rules regarding divorce so as not to encourage this option unless there is no alternative for the couple.

Also, a Muslim man is allowed to marry women from an Abrahamic religion, but Muslim women aren't allowed to marry non-Muslim men.

The ceremonies in Muslim marriage are as follows:

- **Mehr:** The marital contract sometimes has a mehr. This is a statement that the groom will pay a certain amount of money to the bride. This can also be in the form of a gift or any other item.

- **Nikkah:** A Muslim religious scholar recites prayers and verses from the Quran and presents the marriage proposal in front of the groom and bride separately. If they agree, they say "I do". After this confirmation, the couple signs their marriage documents.

- **Blessings:** The officiate blesses the couple and the ceremony is concluded. **Walima:** The groom has to give a dinner after the *nikkah* as a means of sharing his happiness with his guests.

Hinduism

In Hinduism, marriage is treated as a holy duty. According to old Hindu religious literature, the bride and groom did not need any witness to seal their bond. This marriage was referred to as *gandharvavivaha*.

Love marriages and arranged marriages take place in Hinduism, though the religious scholars prefer arranged marriages.

A Hindu marriage mostly takes place after a *pundit* (Hindu religious scholar) has analyzed the *kundlis* (horoscopes) of the bride and groom, and has given his consent.

Ceremonies in a Hindu wedding include:

- **Reception of Baraat:** The bride's family welcomes the groom, his family and guests. The procession is referred to as the *baraat*.

- **Have Milni:** The families of the bride and groom meet each other.

- **Ganesh Puja:** The two families perform a religious ritual known as *ganesh puja*. In this, they worship their God, Ganesha.

- **Bride and Groom Enter the Mandap:** The groom enters the *mandap*, which is a religious altar. The religious scholar recites some prayers after which the bride enters the *mandap*.

- **Exchange of Jai Mala:** The bride and groom exchange floral garlands known as *jai mala*.

- **Kanyadaan:** The bride's father pours water over her hand and places it in the hand of the groom. The groom's sister ties the *saree* (traditional dress) of the bride with the groom's scarf and adds nuts and rice to this knot.

- **Vivahhoma:** The priest lights up the fire and recites religious verses.

- **Panigrahana:** The groom takes the hand of the bride and makes some vows.

- **Shilarohan:** The bride climbs over a small stone and the bride and groom then walk around the fire seven times.

- **Kumkum and Mangalsutra:** The husband then applies *kumkum* on his wife's forehead and puts a beaded necklace known as *mangalsutra* around her neck.

- **Aashirvaad:** The ceremony then concludes and the newlyweds take blessings from their elders.

Sikhism

In Sikhism, marriage is a holy institution. It is referred to as *Anand Karaj*, which means a blissful union. It is a joyous event for the families of the bride and groom. According to the *RehatMaryada*, which is the official Sikh code of conduct, the families of the bride and groom must not give importance to the caste, lineage or race of the bride and groom, and must treat them with respect. However, Sikhism does not allow a Sikh man or woman to marry someone from another faith.

Sikhism does not allow people to refer to horoscopes for marrying someone. The wedding ceremony must be performed only in a *gurdwara*, which is the holy place of worship for Sikhs. The ceremony can take place at any time of the day.

Ceremonies in Sikh weddings are:

- **Milnee:** Families of the bride and groom meet and greet each other.

- **Bride and Groom Sit:** The bride sits on the left side of the groom before Guru Granth Sahib Ji.

- **Prayer:** Guru Granth Sahib Ji performs a prayer to bless the couple.

- **Speech:** The religious scholar gives a speech to explain the importance of marriage

- **Couple Bows:** The couple bows in front of Guru Granth Sahib Ji to honor their commitment.

- **Scarf Placing:** The father of the bride places an end of a scarf in the hand of the groom and then passes it over his shoulder and places the scarf's other side in the hand of the bride.

- **Lavaa:** Guru Granth Sahib Ji then reads different marriage hymns known as *lavaa*. The first *lavaa* talks about the importance of performing their duties.

The second *lavaa* talks about love for one another; the third *lavaa* represents the time of detachment and the fourth *lavaa*symbolizes reunion.

- **Singing Anand Sahib:** The guests then sing stanzas from Anand Sahib, which is a famous song of happiness in Sikhism. The marriage then concludes.

Buddhism

Marriage is considered as a worldly affair in Buddhism and it is not given the status of a sacrament. Buddhist couples must follow the civil rules pertinent to marriage in their country.

Before a Buddhist wedding takes place, the horoscopes of the groom and bride are given to a priest. He analyzes them and fixes a suitable time for the marriage. The Betrothal ceremony takes place in which the bride's maternal uncle sits on a raised platform. The priest recites prayers and presents *madyani*, which is a religious beverage to all the guests.

Normally, a Buddhist wedding ceremony takes place in a temple. The bride and groom enter the temple with their families. They also carry a tray containing ritual fruits and cakes. The bride and groom light candles and bow down to honor the idol of Gautama Buddha. The couple and their families chant religious hymns to conclude the ceremony.

The symbols of marriage in Buddhism are goldfish, abundant food, prayer flags, lotus flower, white scarf, candles, bells and statue of Buddha. These will be looked at closer in a later chapter.

Types of Marriage

The commonly observed types of marriages are:

Heterosexual marriages: Members of the opposite genders marry each other according to the rituals of their religion. This type of marriage is allowed in all the religions; the only condition is usually that the couple belongs to the same faith.

Heterosexual, Interfaith Wedding: A man and woman of different religions get married to each other. This is not acceptable in most religions, but some do allow certain cases of marriages from different religious backgrounds.

Same-sex Marriages: Marrying someone from the same sex is prohibited in almost all the religions. However, the western countries are becoming more open to it, although it is still unacceptable in the many countries.

Polygynous Marriage: A man can marry several women at the same time. This isn't allowed in all religions. The number of wives a man can have is restricted in different religions. For instance, in Islam, a man can only have a maximum of four wives at the same time.

Cohabiting: This relationship is also known as simply living together. In this relationship, a couple does not marry, but lives together as partners. It is forbidden in Islam, Hinduism and Sikhism. Ancient Christianity also prohibits this relationship, but it is now commonly practiced in western countries.

Chapter 2.

Symbols of Marriage

There are different symbols of marriage, according to different cultures and religions.

Symbols of Marriage in the Society

All the symbols discussed below are what different religions perceive to be the signs of a good marriage. However, things are a little different in the real world. The symbols of marriage in the society are quite different than the religious symbols of marriage.

As a kid I was told that marriage is a good thing and a happy couple sitting together with a baby symbolized a happy marriage for me. For a very long time, I believed that having a child with your spouse is a symbol of a happy married life and that is what we all aim for. This is what the society around me conveyed to me. My grandparents communicated the same thing with me. However, when I grew up, gained more sense and became more aware of the good and bad in life, I found out that having a baby in a relationship could be a symbol of marriage for some but not for all.

Secondly, it appears that a married couple with three children might not be living a happy and content life with each other. Who knows they might fight with each other every day and want to get out of the relationship as soon as possible? Children are still perceived as a symbol of marriage, but one should not confuse them with a happy marriage.

Marriage is all about finding your right match and living your life with that person. If you do happen to see Modern Family, which is a great sitcom that airs on ABC channel, then you will understand what I mean. There are three married couples in the show: one gay couple, one straight couple with a husband and wife who are almost the same age and were college sweethearts, another straight couple with a huge age difference between the husband and wife- the wife is even referred to as the husband's daughter in some episodes or even "trophy wife" at some point. All the three couples have their share of pros and cons, and not even one of them is perfect; but all of them have one thing common- the love they have for one another. All the couples love each other and do not want to live apart, and that is what makes their marital lives successful.

You need to look for that thing in your life and make sure your marriage is similar to that of Phil's and Claire's, Gloria's and Jay's, and Cameron's and Mitchell's (they are the characters of the show.)

Finding the perfect Prince Charming should not be your aim because trust me, that is not going to happen. Nobody is perfect, so waiting for your prince Charming to arrive on a beautiful white horse means that you will die alone. Bear this thing clearly in mind and look for someone who is compatible with you. Fairytales do exhibit marriage as a perfect thing and that one does find their Prince Charming, or Snow White, but these ideals are only restricted to fantasies.

Life isn't a fantasy and the sooner you bear that in mind, the easier it will become for you to get a clear idea about marriage and find a suitable mate.

Symbols of Marriage in Christianity

There are several symbols of marriage in Christianity. Some of the commonly practiced ones are as follows.

- **Carrying something old, new, borrowed and blue:** On her wedding day, the bride must carry something old, something new, something borrowed and something blue. This tradition dates back to Victorian times and is derived from a famous and old English rhyme: "*Something* old, *something new, something borrowed, something blue, a sixpence in your shoe.*" The bride should have some old piece that belonged to her family to represent her old life; something new, as it is a symbol of her life with her spouse in the future; a borrowed item from a married woman who is happy in her life as that object will help the new bride to be really happy in her marital life as well; and she should also have something colored in blue, as it symbolizes constancy and fidelity.

- **Wearing white gown:** Christian brides normally wear a white bridal dress. Queen Victoria who chose to wear a white gown instead of a silver one on her wedding day incepted this tradition. White signifies virginity and purity, and is said to help ward off the evil spirits.

- **Throwing rice:** The newlywed couple is showered with grains of rice as it symbolizes fertility.

- **Wedding cake:** Having a cake on the wedding originates from Roman times. During those days, a cake of food was crushed over the bride to shower her with good luck. Wedding cakes symbolize fertility and good fortune. People who eat the wedding cake will also benefit from its good luck. The bride normally cuts the cake's first slice to bring good fortune to her marriage. The couple eats the cake's first slice together as it is believed it will create a special bond between them. Some brides also place aside one slice of the cake to make sure her other half will remain sincere to her. According to another tradition, if a single woman takes a slice of the wedding cake home with her and places it beneath her pillow, she will see dreams of her future spouse.

- **Ceremonial kiss:** The bride and groom kiss when the priest pronounces them husband and wife. The ceremonial kiss consummates the wedding and joins their souls. It is also observed as a seal that will keep them dedicated to their commitment.

- **Wedding rings:** The married couple wears wedding bands that symbolize God's never-ending love. The bands are circular and a circle has no end, so wearing the wedding rings will bring God's love to that marriage and will keep the couple entwined in each other's love. According to the ancient Egyptian tradition, the wedding bands must be worn by the bride and groom on their left hand's third finger as the vein of affection and love runs directly from that point to your heart. Hence, placing a ring on that finger denotes eternal love.

- **Groom wears a boutonniere:** Grooms wear boutonniere on their weddings to prove their love to their brides. Boutonnieres are also given to the guests on some weddings to bring them good luck.

- **Bridal bouquet:** Flowers are a popular symbol of fecundity and sex. The bride carries a bouquet to represent fruitfulness. Ribbons tied around the bouquet represent good luck.

- **Bridal veil:** The bride wears a veil on her wedding. This represents several things. Many people believe that wearing a veil on the wedding day will protect the bride from all kinds of evil spirits. Other sources indicate that wearing a veil represents that the bride is submitting herself to her better half. A few sources also state that veil signifies the love the bride has for her husband.

- **Honeymoon:** This word is derived from the Teuton (ancient Germanic tribe) practice in which a person drinks mead for 30 days after their wedding. Mead is a wine that is made with honey. The newlywed couple goes on a honeymoon as a celebration of their marriage.

- **Horseshoe:** A horseshoe is presented to the newlywed couple to wish them with good fortune and good luck

Symbols of Marriage in Judaism

Most of the symbols of marriage in Judaism are similar to that observed in Christianity. Some of the unique ones are:

- **Ketubah signing:** Before the wedding ceremony is commenced, the groom takes an object given to him by the holy rabbi, lifts it, and then returns it. He then signs the Ketubah and takes an oath that he will love and support his wife.

- **Going to the chuppah:** After signing the Ketubah, the groom goes to the Chuppah that symbolizes the house he will provide to his bride.

- **Wine and glass breaking:** The rabbi blesses the newlywed couple over a glass of wine. The married couple drinks wine from that glass. After drinking the wine, the couple breaks it, as it is believed the shards of the broken glass will bring them good luck.

- **Unity candle:** A unity candle is lit at the wedding ceremony to wish the bride and groom a married life full of light and happiness.

Symbols of Marriage in Buddhism

There are no standard symbols of marriage in Buddhism. These symbols vary from one Buddhist country to another. However, the following symbols are normally seen on most of the Buddhist wedding ceremonies:

- **Photos of dear ones:** Photographs of the loved ones of the newly married couple are normally placed during their wedding ceremony to symbolize respect, honor and love.

- **Prayer flags and incense:** These are used in the wedding ceremony to shower blessings on the married couple.

- **Vegetarian food:** Some Buddhist couples have a vegetarian menu on their wedding to demonstrate gratefulness.

- **Abundant food:** You will often see an overabundance of delicious food in Buddhist weddings as it signifies generosity. Newlywed couples also make charitable donations to bring happiness in their marital life.

- **Goldfish:** Some Buddhist couple also bring goldfish to their wedding as this symbolizes happiness and joy.

- **Lotus flower, bells and candles:** These objects are also normally seen on the majority of the Buddhist weddings as they represent wisdom and a transformation of the couple from single to married.

Symbols of Marriage in Hinduism

The common and popular symbols of marriage in Hinduism are listed below.

- **Sindoor:** During the wedding ceremony, the groom applies *sindoor* (vermillion) on his bride's head, at the point where her hair parts. During the entire course of her marriage, the bride wears *sindoor*. It is a symbol of the goddess *Parvati's* flame and it is believed that it gives power to the married woman.

- **Mangalsutra:** The married woman also wears a beaded necklace known as "mangalsutra". It protects the couple from evil eye.

- **Toe rings:** Most Hindu married women wear toe rings to serve as a reminder of their devotion to their husbands; it is so they never resort to infidelity.

- **Wearing bangles:** A married Hindu woman must always wear bangles to symbolize that she is a happily married woman.

- **White scarf, endless knot and red string:** These items signify connectedness and a strong bond between the bride and groom. A white scarf with water is also used as a symbol of purity.

- **Buddha statue:** A statue of the Buddha is also placed during the wedding ceremony to protect the married couple from evil eye and spirits.

Symbols of Marriage in Islam

Some Islamic symbols of marriage as:

- **Marriage Sermon:** This sermon is referred to as "khutba-tun-nikah". It is a sermon given by a religious scholar of the Muslim community in order to bless the newly married couple and bring them lots of happiness and good fortune in their marital life.

- **HaqMehr:** The groom gives a certain amount of money to his bride. This sum is decided by the bride or her family, or due to a joint agreement between the families of the groom and bride. Haqmehr is a symbol of the groom's commitment towards his bride and that he will work hard to provide for her. It can also be in the form of a gift, property or any other thing that the bride wishes to have.

- **Walima ceremony:** The "walima" is basically an event in which the groom gives dinner to all his relatives, friends and other guests. It can take place immediately after the marriage ceremony, or any other day as decided by the groom. It is a means of celebrating his happiness and taking home his new bride.

The basic purpose of all these symbols is to shower good luck and happiness on the newly married couple, and it is not compulsory for you to observe them.

Chapter 3.

Traditions, Superstitions and Facts

There are lots of interesting facts, traditions and superstitions associated with marriage. Take a look at some of them below.

Facts about Marriage:

- The word "marriage" is derived from the word "mas". It is a Latin word that means masculine or male. The earliest use of the word marriages dates back to the early 13th century.

- On average, a married couple only spends a mere four minutes per day together alone. This is mainly due to the responsibilities, household chores, kids, television, jobs and other activities the couple has to perform.

- The Talmud takes marriage very seriously and has banned extramarital affairs and sex. It also has created a timetable regarding how often spouses should indulge in sexual activities with their better halves. A man living independently on his own should rejoice his wife daily, a laborer should enjoy sex with his wife two times a week, riders of donkeys should do it only once per week, camel drivers should do it once a month, and sailors should indulge in such acts twice a year.

- People who marry before they reach 25 have a higher risk of experiencing divorce than those who marry at 25 or above.

- Over 75% of people who marry partners from an affair eventually divorce

- No sex in a marriage has a much more powerful negative impact on a marriage than good sex has a positive impact.

- The cost of an average wedding is $20,000. The cost of an average divorce is $20,000

- Compared to singles, married people accumulate about four times more savings and assets. Those who divorced had assets 77% lower than singles

- The probability of a first marriage ending in a divorce within 5 years is 20%, but the probability of a premarital cohabitation breaking up within 5 years is 49%. After 10 years, the probability of a first marriage ending is 33%, compared with 62% for cohabitations

- If an older woman marries a younger man, the marriage is likely to end in divorce.

- The longest marriage ever registered is 91 years and 12 days

- There are apparently more than 190 reasons to get married

- On average, a married couple has sex around 58 times per year, which is more than doing it once per week.

- The word "husband" is derived from the word "husbondi", which is a word of the famous Old Norse language that means "the house's master". Some sources state that the word "groom" is derived from the word "guma", which is an Old English word meaning "man".

- A person's level of education is linked to the age of their marriage. People with higher education tend to marry late.

- 80 per cent of all the marriages that took place in the past were between close relatives or second cousins.

- In France, people are allowed to marry deceased individuals.

- There is a colony in New York named Oneida, which was set up in 1848. It advocated group marriage, otherwise known as complex marriage, and enforced it upon every woman; this meant that every woman in the community was married to every male. The Oneida also practiced scientific breeding.

- Approximately 300 couples are married in Las Vegas every day.

- In China 26,000 couples get married ever day

- A 96-year-old woman was divorced by her 99-year-old husband because he found out she had a serious affair during the 1940s.

- The first recorded mention of same-sex marriage occurs in Ancient Rome and seems to have occurred without too much debate until Christianity became the official religion. In 1989, Denmark was the first post-Christianity nation to legally recognize same-sex marriage

- The largest wedding attendance was a Jewish wedding in Jerusalem in 1993 where 30,000 people attended.

- A Malaysian man holds the record for being the best man at over 1000 weddings

- Most expensive wedding ever? The marriage of Sheik Rashid Bin Saeed Al Maktoum's son to Princess Salama in Dubai in May 1981. The price tag? $44 million

- In Japan, white was always the color of choice for bridal ensembles -- long before Queen Victoria popularized it in the Western world

Superstitions and Traditions Related to Marriage

There are many superstitions related to marriage, some of which may seem really strange.

- According to Greek tradition, a bride who wants a sweet marriage should tuck a cube of sugar into her gloves.

- According to an English tradition, the finest day to get married is Wednesday and the worst or unluckiest day for marriage is Saturday. Although Monday is for wealth and Tuesday is for health.

- According to Hindu tradition, rain on a wedding day is a sign of good luck.

- Ancient Romans used to study pig entrails for determining the best time to get married.

- If you want to safeguard yourself from curses and evil eye, then paint your feet and hands with henna on your wedding day, as per the Middle Eastern traditions.

- According to Italian tradition, both the groom and the bride should break one glass on their wedding day. The more the shards of the glass, the more happy years that will be enjoyed by the married couple.

- As good luck, an Egyptian bride is pinched numerous times on her big day.

- Czechs throw peas instead of grains of rice on the newlyweds.

- According to a famous English legend, finding a spider in your dress before walking down the aisle is a good omen.

- Another outrageous wedding superstition states that if you let a cat devour food from your left shoe almost a week before your wedding day, and then you're most likely to have a successful marriage.

- According to a Finnish tradition, brides should go door-to-door and collect wedding gifts in their pillowcase and they should be escorted by a much older married man to ensure a happy married life of their own.

- In Morocco, women bathe in milk before their marriage ceremony in order to cleanse their bodies.

- Dropping your wedding bands on your wedding day is a sign of death. Whoever of the two drops the ring first is bound to welcome death soon.

- According to a Roman tradition, wearing veil on the wedding day protects the bride from all sorts of bad luck and evil spirits.

- Wearing a white dress on the wedding day is considered as a huge omen of good luck. Wearing red signifies inviting death, though in the Indian subcontinent and Asian countries, wearing red by the brides on their big day is a symbol of good luck and prosperity.

- Another superstition states that if you wish to be the dominant one in your marriage, then you must make a hefty purchase before your spouse-to-be makes one.

- According to a strange Tudor custom, it is okay for people to pelt shoes at the newlyweds, as this tradition will bring them good luck.

- In Asia, wearing robes with embroidered cranes symbolizes fidelity for the length of a marriage

- An old wives' talc: If the younger of two sisters marries first, the older sister must dance barefoot at the wedding or risk never landing a husband

- The bride stands to the groom's left during a Christian ceremony, because in bygone days the groom needed his right hand free to fight off other suitors.

- February 10th is World Marriage Day

- Life in the 1500's: Most people got married in June because they took their yearly bath in May and were still smelling pretty good by June. However, they were starting to smell, so brides carried a bouquet of flowers to hide the body odor.

- In Holland, a pine tree is planted outside the newlyweds' home as a symbol of fertility and luck

- If a cat sneezes on the day before a wedding, the bride will be lucky in her marriage

- A young bride would wear her hair long and loose as a symbol of her youth and innocence

- The custom of carrying the bride over the threshold stems from the same belief that aroused the idea of runway carpet and strewing the aisle with flowers and petals. It was an ancient belief that the newly married couple was very susceptible to evil spirits. By carrying the bride and supplying a protective layer between the floor and bride, she would be protected from the ground monster

Chapter 4

Don't Do It for the Wrong Reasons

Marriage is, unarguably, one of the largest milestones in any person's life. Alongside the dependence and support that married couples are expected to provide to each other, it also comes with a whole list of responsibilities and emotions. Although marriage can have numerous benefits, such as financial support and relative economic stability, it is a decision that should never be jumped into blindly.

Taxation Benefits

One major benefit, which is probably also the least romantic, is regarding taxes. In many countries all over the world, married partners can file for joint tax returns. This means that a spouse with a lower income rate can allow the other to take the benefit of falling into a combined lower-tax bracket. Spouses also provide tax-free havens where things like gifts and property can be exchanged without additional taxes. Governments to encourage the institution of marriage have introduced taxation benefits and deductions, but in no situation should any citizen get married solely to benefit their tax returns.

Financial Support

Historically, financial support has been one of the main reasons for the existence of many marriages. In ancient times, whilst women bore and nestled offspring, it was the man's job to hunt food and provide for the family. This allowed for the survival of the weaker members of the pack and ultimately led to the structure of the modern nuclear family. However, in modern times, greater emphasis has been placed on creating financial parity between the genders. This is mostly seen in developed western countries. This is not to discourage marriage itself, but to give the partners an equal footing. Still, it is safe to say that with two earning members in a marriage, there is a greater amount of shared disposable income and spending power. This also leads to a better standard of living and a safety net if one member loses their income for any reason.

Laws of inheritance and insurance policies are measurable in favor of marriage; they encourage most people to legalize the relationship they have with their loved ones. As written by John Kenney in an article for Esquire Magazine, "If I got hit by a bus tomorrow, would Mary lose out financially simply because she was my wife in everything except name? Well, it turned out, yes, she would. And I couldn't bear that." The author later wrote about finally getting married to his partner of 20 years just for this reason.

A key point here is that legalities like prenuptial agreements are fast gaining popularity. These allow for spouses to provide financially for spouses as they deem fit. In most cases, individuals are not legally bound to provide financial support for spouses and do so purely out of personal consideration.

Peer, family or societal pressure

Society has long been blamed for pressurizing people into marriage. It can be argued that family and peers, being active members of society, are influenced by its beliefs. Thus, they may outwardly or unknowingly pressurize those around them. These influences seem mostly harmless until they are strictly enacted upon.

Marriage should be a choice, a personal one for the people involved.

For women in particular, the "biological clock syndrome" is one of the greatest pressures there is; it isn't induced by a nagging mother or fussy friend, but by nature itself. If a woman happens to want a traditional family and children, she has to work for it within a biological timeframe. Many women base their marriage decisions on actions compromised by the ticking clock.

Ariel, a 36-year-old divorced mother of two, writes in her book titled Offbeat Bride: "I feel those pressures weighing down on me. I can only imagine how paralyzing it could be for younger women. It paralyzed me into passivity. I honor all the women here for consciously choosing their own vision, of making their wedding, their marriage, as an act of freedom, not conformity."

Impressing others

We've often heard that spouses are meant to complement one another and there is no serious wrong in recognizing the impressive qualities of your spouse. Often, people fall for the image of trophy wives and perfect husbands in order to please the people around them, rather than their own intrinsic side. We thrive in meeting the approval of others, but it is primarily important to meet our spouse's approval, and vice versa.

Saving a relationship

It is believed that, more often than not, partners may feel threatened in their relationship. Believing that a partner may be unfaithful or leave at whim without the presence of any social or legal obligations may drive the other to demand a legally binding marriage. Recent statistics disagree with the idea that marriage acts as a detriment to actions that otherwise threaten the relationship between a couples. For example, a study conducted in 1991 by sex researcher Shere Hite found that 70% of married women had cheated on their partners. A similar study conducted in 1993 showed that 72% of married men had also been unfaithful. Some go as far to argue that marriage sours a relationship and those choosing to stay in a relationship despite the absence of a legally binding contract are relatively happier.

Another theory is based on the belief that nothing, not even a relationship, stays constant. Everything needs to change, grow and develop, or it will eventually die. Marriage seems to be the logical next step in any developed relationship, allowing it to enter the next level of social and legal commitment and a new phase in its existence.

Forced by partner

A number of forced marriages take place every year, mostly in poor underdeveloped nations. Women are bought and sold as wives and, in many cases, even children are subjected to dissenting unions. The victims may not have the ability or the means to file for divorce, so the marriages are continued.

In the developed world, slavery into marriage is rare. Still, partners may pressurize or even threaten the other into an unconsented marriage. This practice is an offence with legal repercussions.

Simply put, the start to a marriage is often given a lot of importance as it is the wedding ceremony itself. In all cultures, it is a moment of celebration and often one of great emotional and financial weight. What is important to note is that the end to a marriage, though opposite in nature, is also one packed with emotional stress and great financial cost. The end of a marriage is an upheaval of a lifestyle where each member of the communion has to once more begin a life separate from the other. Therefore, it is safe to presume that the institution of marriage should not be entered in for the "wrong" reasons or at least those not strong enough to face the challenges that lie ahead.

Chapter 5.

Reasons to Get Married

Aside from falling in love with what seems to be the perfect partner for you, there are many reasons that may encourage an individual to turn towards marriage. In fact you could potentially find more than **190** different reasons to get married. For many people, marriage is not entirely about love; it is more about holding up commitment and starting a family. Marriage may even seem to be an appropriate way of improving income and raising status.

Let's explore some of the major reasons to get married and delve deeper into each one.

Commitment, Attachment and Stability

The yearning for attachment and stability in life is what drives many people to get married. Everyone wants to have a comfortable and stable living where they can enjoy life peacefully with a loving partner. By getting married, one is able to acquire some steadiness in life with the help of their spouse. As marriage is a commitment with each other; both the spouses are able to receive mutual attachment and affection.

As quoted by famous English entertainer and presenter, Bruce Forsyth, "The secret to a happy marriage is if you can be at peace with someone within four walls, if you are content because the one you love is near to you, either upstairs or downstairs, or in the same room, and you feel that warmth that you don't find very often, then that is what love is all about."

This shows that marriage does bring with it an element of closeness, compassion and warmth to fill up your heart and life with love, helping you live a more relaxed and complete life than when you were alone.

Financial Benefit

Attaining attachment and stability in life isn't the only reason why people get married. Some people make this decision to enjoy the financial benefits associated with marriage.

Married couples are able to build up a lot more wealth than cohabiting couples or single people. One reason is that when both partners in a marriage are working and earning money, the average income is automatically higher. Another reason is that married couples are also able to hoard money better than single people. Single people often have the habit of wasting money, which results in a decrease in their net worth with time. A study showed that married men with similar abilities and education as unmarried men are able to make 20 percent more money than the latter.

Married men also have better employment status than cohabiting or single men. A reason behind this could be the way the society views married men. Married men are generally considered to be more hardworking and honest than unmarried men, which is why their chances of getting better jobs are increased. The productivity of men is also somewhat dependent on their married life as the efficiency and output of married men is likely to rise by 27 percent, as compared to when they were unmarried. Married people also have less chances of suffering from poverty than unmarried people.

Marriage results in the increase in the number of family members, which obviously produces an increase in the needs of the family. These needs motivate more family members to work and earn for the family, thus resulting in an enhancement in the total family income. A study showed that marriage produces approximately a nine per cent yearly increase in the family income.

In addition to that, married people are also able to reap the benefits of discount packages and deals. While applying for a loan, homeowner's insurance, or buying a car, a married couple is more likely to get better rates, concessions, discounts and offers than an unmarried couple. Secondly, married families are also given significant reductions in their yearly taxes. This benefit is often not provided to single people or cohabiting couples.

Married couples also tend to make their individual retirement accounts (IRAs). If one of the spouses makes this account, then both partners will enjoy its benefits. IRA payments are often difficult to pay for single couples, but married people can make the most of them.

Also, if any spouse is suffering from a business loss, then the other spouse can use that reason to get a write-off in their annual taxes. Hence, financial losses suffered by married people can bring them certain financial reliefs as well.

Marriage also helps in boosting your credit ranking. As married couples are preferred by banks and other financial institutions, they are easily able to get the loans they apply for, which certainly improves their credit scores. This is because married couples are viewed as more trustworthy and stable by the society and the financial institutions, when compared to single people.

Moreover, marriage can also help you protect your estate. When a married person dies, their assets are passed on to their spouse (as per their will) and no estate tax will be generated on the assets. This exemption helps safeguard the estate of the deceased until their spouse passes away.

Another financial benefit gained by married couples is "benefit-shop". This refers to the benefits they enjoy from their salary packages. If one spouse enjoys better benefits, then the other can reap them as well. For instance, if one spouse receives medical allowance from their firm, then the other can also enjoy the medical allowance and is able to save more money.

Marriage can also bring a big reduction in the charitable contributions that you need to make every year. If your spouse makes an enormous contribution, but doesn't have enough income equivalent to the double of that particular amount, then the additional contribution is carried over. If a married couple has filed for the contributions together, then they can determine the deductible amount of the contributions by analyzing their incomes.

Sexual Satisfaction

Married couples are also more sexually satisfied than the unmarried and have a more peaceful sex life. This is due to the availability and commitment of their sexual partner. A 2006 study conducted by British researchers investigated the sexual behaviors and habits of several men in about 38 countries. The study revealed that all the married men, regardless of their residence, had more sex than their unmarried counterparts.

In addition, married couples in monogamous relationships have more sexual satisfaction than unmarried, cohabiting or single people.

Frequent sex also results in more sexual satisfaction, which can help in reducing tension and stress. As married people can indulge in sexual activities more often, they are able to enjoy their benefits more easily as well.

In addition to that, marriage also brings an element of fidelity and loyalty in the relationship. Spouses tend to trust each other more than cohabiters, which improves their sexual performance and results in higher levels of satisfaction.

Healthy Lifestyle

It is often observed that married people tend to have a more healthy and happy life than single or cohabiting people; a married couple is able to stay in a better physical and mental shape than single people. This is because married couples can constantly depend on and care for their spouse.

If one partner in a marriage is sick, the other one can ensure prompt and thorough medical care. However, a single person who is living alone is unable to enjoy these little benefits and loving moments, which could result in the deterioration of health.

Moreover, most married couples have children and, when they grow older, their children are usually present to take care of them. This is why married parents tend to have a much better physical health than single people.

A few studies have shown that a married woman is able to live a healthier, happier and stress-free life compared to that of a single or divorced woman, or one who is going through separation with her spouse. Also, a married mother is less prone to common ailments like fever, flu, cough and cold than a single mother. The longer a woman stays married, the less are her chances of acquiring different diseases and medical conditions. This is because marriage tends to reinforce the immune system and fortify it. Married couples have a good impact on each other's immune system; it becomes more stimulated, thereby helping the person to combat certain illnesses.

A Norwegian research study showed that never-married and divorced men who were cancer victims had about 11 per cent and 16 per cent higher death rates, respectively, when compared to married men who were suffering from cancer. Another eight-year-study carried out in UCLA revealed that people in good health had an 88 per cent chance of dying during the period of that study if they remained single.

Marriage also tends to increase longevity. As married people have less chances of becoming sick, they are able to stay in a good shape, which increases their average life. In addition to that, a married couple is able to maintain a healthier weight; this helps in decreasing their chances of acquiring diseases caused by obesity, such as diabetes and cardiac problems. When the risk of these diseases and conditions is reduced, the longevity of the couple naturally increases.

Married couples also engage in a lot of physical activity than unmarried couples. Physical activity is directly associated with a better physical and mental health because the more you exercise or participate in vigorous activities, the more that stress is released from your body. The release of toxins and stress enhances both your mood and your health, thus resulting in a prolonged and happier life.

The health of married couples also tends to improve because people committed in a marital relationship have less likelihood of indulging in alcoholism and drug abuse. Various studies clearly revealed that marriage promotes a reduction in the use of drugs and alcohol.

A major reason behind this shift is that married couples either drink less or drink after a longer period than the single individuals or cohabiting couples. Also, a single person is likely to decrease the amount of drugs or alcohol they consume after getting married. Married people have less time to spare for drinking; they become more mature and experience a strong sense of responsibility and commitment, which is why they often drink much less.

According to the National Institute on Alcohol Abuse and Alcoholism (NIAAA), around 56 percent of married people abstain from drinking, 20 percent of married couples are light drinkers, 15 percent are moderate drinkers, and only 6 percent are heavy drinkers.

About 35 percent of cohabiting couples are abstainers, 24 percent are light drinkers, 24 percent are moderate drinkers, and only 15 percent are heavy drinkers. Approximately 80 percent of widowed women abstain from drinking while 9 percent are light drinkers, 7 percent moderately indulge in drinking, and 3 percent are heavy drinkers.

Furthermore, 54 percent of separated individuals abstain from drinking alcohol, 18 percent are light alcohol users, 15 percent moderately drink, and 10 percent are heavy alcohol drinkers. About 52 percent of divorced people are abstainers of alcohol, 19 percent are light drinkers, 18 percent are moderate drinkers, and 10 percent are heavy drinkers of alcohol. On the other hand, amongst the people who have never married, 47 percent of them abstain from drinking alcohol, 18 percent are light users of alcohol, 23 percent are moderate drinkers, and 10 percent are heavy drinkers.

These statistics exhibit that a vast majority of the married people abstain from drinking, whereas the percentage of alcohol abstainers is less amongst the individuals involved in a cohabiting relationship or those who never married.

It also shows that divorce can lure a person into alcoholism. The intimacy and commitment restraints are no longer present after a person is divorced, which is why they are likely to get inclined towards this behavior and seek it as a means of venting out their frustration.

Marriage also positively affects an individual's habit of substance abuse. A study exhibited that the change from being unmarried to married also resulted in a huge decrease in the use of marijuana. People who remained committed to their spouse throughout their life hardly consumed marijuana. On the contrary, those who married and later divorced or separated from their spouse showed an escalating shift towards marijuana abuse.

Moreover, it was also observed that people who married alcoholics or marijuana users were most likely to live a life of depression and tension. Their chances of becoming alcoholics or addicts also rose sharply, and it was seen that if these couples had children, then they were most likely to become addicts in some point of their life.

Furthermore, marriage also improves the mental health and mood swings of people. Married couples are able to share their feelings with each other and tend to treat each other with love, care and respect. These emotions reduce their stress and promote a boost in the release of endorphins in their bodies. Endorphins are hormones associated with happiness. With more endorphins swimming in your body, your mood tends to brighten up. This is why married people suffer from far less depression, stress and anxiety than unmarried people or cohabiting couples.

In a study conducted published in the Journal of Health and Social Behavior 49(3) in 2008, about 1.1 million people were studied in a period of 32 years – from 1972 until 2003. The study showed that men who never married in 1972 had extremely low life expectancy, as compared to those who were married once in their life or those who had a long marriage. A major reason behind this is that married men during the 1970s had the support of their wives. Their wives used to take care of them and make sure they were in a good physical state. Men who never married could not enjoy the compassion offered by a loving partner, which is why they had a lower life expectancy than the married ones.

The study also observed the lives of different widows and found out the widows who were married during the 1970s experienced a seven per cent decrease in their health after their better halves left them alone in this world.

Another thing noticed by most researchers is that the duration of a marriage has some relation to the mortality rate of the married people. The longer a marriage lasts, the lower that the mortality rate and risks suffered by that married couple will be.

Societal Benefits

There is a certain population of people that becomes inclined towards the idea of saying "I do" to someone in order to benefit partly from the societal advantages. One of the biggest societal benefits of marriage is the way that the society perceives you. A married person is more likely to gain the respect their peers than a single person, particularly in conservative places.

In addition to that, married couples enjoy benefits such as getting a better house, reductions in different society contributions, and major deals. Moreover, married women also have lower risks of being sexually exploited or raped than single women. About 46 percent of unmarried women are forced into sexual activities whereas only 9 percent of married women go through this trauma. This shows that the chances of married women being sexually abused are far less than that of single women.

Domestic violence has also been observed more in people in cohabiting relationships than in married couples. This means that a married woman is most likely to be able to avoid domestic violence.

A married couple experiencing an argument or a fight won't always resort to physical attacks, as compared to an unmarried couple. This maybe because married couples share more intimacy towards one another and respect each other more. Furthermore, they realize that marriage is a strong bond and that their violent act might result in the death of that relationship, which is why they avoid relying on violent measures to express their disagreement and fury. On the contrary, unmarried or cohabiting couples are not obligated to live together, which is why they can easily take the aide of any violent measures. It may also be because two people entering the legal contract of marriage are unlikely to do so if their partner is violent or abusive; this may be observed less in the context of cohabitation.

A major societal benefit linked with marriage is a reduction in the crime rate of a community. The chances of married couples committing a small to heinous crime are quite less than that of single people or those in cohabiting relationships.

Studies have also proven that boys raised by single parents have a higher tendency of engaging in aberrant behavior, as compared to boys raised by biological married parents. A reason behind this surge of delinquent demeanor could be the lack of security offered by the single parent to their son.

On the other hand, marriage is a beautiful institution that creates a better environment for the children to be raised in, thus resulting in more focused, friendly and well-mannered children. Of course, both these statements cannot be generalized and there are cases in which children raised by responsible, affectionate and educated married parents often indulge in undesirable acts and do not realize or appreciate their social responsibilities and vice versa.

Family Life, Parenting and Having Children

Marriage also provides you with the chance of having biological children and starting your own family.

Children raised by both biological parents have fewer chances of suffering from poverty and economic insecurity. They also tend to stay longer in school, experience less behavioral problems, and are far less susceptible to severe emotional and physical conditions than those raised by single, divorced, separated or remarried parents.

Generally, children of single or divorced parents show a strong bitterness towards marriage and other forms of commitment. On the other hand, children nurtured by married couples show a positive attitude towards commitment and marriage and are more likely to have a successful marriage.

Education

Another benefit of marriage is being able to provide your children with good education. Married couples tend to provide more valuable help to their kids with homework and other academic activities than single or divorced parents. Biological fathers are also known to show more interest in the education of their children than the step-fathers.

In addition to the above, children belonging to married couples show better performance in school and are less likely to drop out of school at a young age than the children of single or divorced people.

Chapter 6.

Is It For Me?

Traditional views in most societies were eminently pro-marriage. Not only was it encouraged in religious spheres, but also as a form of societal control. The concept of Adam and Eve was conditioned on the belief that a man and woman belong together and people were taught that being married was how God intended humans to "go forth and be fruitful".

Men and women, it is argued, were created to complete one another, to provide support both physical and emotional support, and to form a legalized union that was conducive to bearing and raising children. However, throughout history, the main reason individuals married was that they believed that it was beneficial. Men and women are, like many other members of the animal kingdom, physically and emotionally attracted to each other. In essence, even in olden times, love and longing was as much to blame for the establishing of marriage as was any other external factor.

In the modern world, many believe that the factors that made marriage so essential have altered, now blurring the lines between benefit and detriment. In principle, women's liberation has led to them no longer being financially dependent on men, and with the rise in adoption and surrogates, they do not need a men physically to have children either; both can live fairly wholesome and successful lives apart, but yet will always have deep down a feeling of incompletion.

Concept of commitment

Homer, the famed Greek philosopher, wrote of marriage: "There is nothing nobler or more admirable than when two people who see eye to eye keep house as man and wife, confounding their enemies and delighting their friends." The quote, written centuries ago, represents what most want from a modern-day marriage.

Often, you'll hear people talk of committing to one another, but many fail to recognize that marriage is an entity to which both members need to commit. According to a recent study, approximately 85% of divorced couples in the United States indicated a lack of commitment to the marriage at each other as the reason they got divorced. Commitment eliminates fears such as neglect and abandonment and allows the couple to work towards the future, rather than just dwell on the present problems they face.

Avoidance of commitment

Many choose to avoid marriage to avoid monogamy, a certain lifestyle, or even a cliché. Others may choose to avoid committing due to certain external factors that may be beyond their control. In any situation, marriage should be considered a choice and those who cannot or do not wish to commit to it should step far away from it.

In many instances, however, individuals are willing to commit to a relationship or person that they deem fit. They may change their views or their feelings may alter according to the circumstances. Many people break up with their significant others over their failure to commit themselves into a marriage; sooner enough, it is seen that they have managed to settle down with another person.

For those whose singular reason to avoid commitment is the fear of losing their freedom, Madeleine L'Engle a recognized writer, writes: "If we commit ourselves to one person for life, this is not, as many people think, a rejection of freedom; rather, it demands the courage to move into all the risks of freedom, and the risk of love which is permanent; into that love which is not possession but participation".

Desire for a Single Lifestyle

Marriage is often associated with responsibility and a certain way of living. Though true to a large extent, marriage has been evolving with time and has taken on a modern face that is quite different to how it was traditionally viewed in the previous years. Traditionally, men used to provide whereas women looked after the house and children. A modern marriage is a lot more open and may consist for example of a married couple who travels around the world together instead of building a home in one place or of a career-oriented woman and a stay-at-home dad.

In many cases, what is important is to find like-minded partners, they can indulge in any style of living they choose, although there are some exceptions to this clause. Firstly, there are some legal requirements and boundaries that individual must observed. For instance, in many cases a man cannot choose to exclude his wife or children from his will and he cannot choose to not give his biological children his name.

Strong fears of divorce

It is believed (not always…) that marriages are essentially much easier to start than end. Divorces are often messy affairs that are emotionally exhausting and financially wrecking for the couple and the people around them, in particularly their children.

Married people naturally fear divorce as it means the end of a relationship, the end of a way of life they have carefully built, and an uncertainty of the future. It is likely that the longer and more successful a marriage is, the harder it will be to end. Assets accumulated over the years, savings, and even children would have to be divided fairly.

The crippling statistics of divorce and infidelity have affected single people greatly. Recent generation, bearing the impact of the rising divorce rate amongst their parents, is skeptical of whether they wish to go through the same ordeal. Societal norms and laws have also developed in favor of unmarried members of society that enable them to live a life of their choice whilst remaining single. Same-sex relationships are on the rise, as are live-in relationships, both eliminating the need for a traditional marriage.

Whatever the reason, marriage seems to be in decline in most of the western world. In an article written by Steven Swinford for the UK Telegraph, he states, "According to the 2011 Census, the number of people who are married in England and Wales has fallen from just over half of the population a decade ago to 45 per cent. The figures represented the first time since the Census was founded in 1801 that married couples have been in a minority."

Balancing marriage with career life

People associate marriage with responsibilities. Though it is true that living together means that chores can be divided and someone may cook your meals and help with the laundry, there is a lot more emotional responsibility on a person who now has others to look after and support.

A website titled For Your Marriage states, "The rub for married couples is when career decisions of one spouse conflict or compete with the marriage, family responsibilities, or the career of the other spouse. It's a matter of discernment and juggling. The balancing act is often not easy."

Even companies recognize that a single person can effectively put in more hours at work, work holidays and overtime simply because they don't have a family waiting for them back home. Asking a single female co-worker to work Christmas morning is bound to be easier than asking a married mother of two to do the same.

At Forbes, Micheal Noer writes about how statistics show that marrying career women is not the ideal marriage to have. He writes, "If a host of studies are to be believed, marrying these women is asking for trouble. If they quit their jobs and stay home with the kids, they will be unhappy (Journal of Marriage and Family, 2003). They will be unhappy if they make more money than you do (Social Forces, 2006). You will be unhappy if they make more money than you do (Journal of Marriage and Family, 2001). You will be more likely to fall ill (American Journal of Sociology). Even your house will be dirtier (Institute for Social Research)."

Similarly for men, women have written scores of books about being married to the workaholic husband. A great career may make for a great salary, but not necessarily a happy wife. Though comical in his tone and igniting the fury of many feminists, Noer recognizes that careers and marriages are a delicate balancing act between water and oil.

Desiring Multiple Relationships

It was traditionally believed that men are not designed to be monogamous creatures and subsequently the modern form of marriage does not suit them. Many societies around the world and even some religions allow for polygamous marriages to this day. However, in most such marriages, it is the men rather than the women who are allowed to keep multiple partners.

A new world viewpoint has been surfacing in which women and men alike are being recognized as non-monogamous beings. The argument is that even in marriage there is a large majority of men and women, who, despite loving their significant others, would not hesitate to be in a non-consequence relationship with another. Infidelity is increasingly being recognized not as a resultant of an unhappy or failed marriage, but as a means of personal fulfillment.

A new relationship provides excitement whilst each partner or lover offers something new that the other may not have. However, the downside is that such relationships are often ruled by uncertainty, jealousy, and a marked competitiveness.

There are some who thrive in marriage and its monogenic structure. There is a bond of trust, familiarity and ownership that comes with being exclusively tied to one another. Psychologists say it is in this uncompetitive, familiarized environment that many feel most comfortable and are able to perform to their best ability in other spheres of life.

If one is wondering if marriage is for them, there are some fundamental questions that they have to ask themselves. The first and the most important one being, "Does getting married with this person will help me achieve all that I would want from marriage?" This question recognizes that marriage can mean many different things to different people. As there is no right or wrong answer, one must recognize what they want from this union and whether getting married is going to enable them to achieve all that. One way of doing so is finding common ground with a prospective spouse. The next chapter will help you to go through more in depth on the process of decision.

As pertinently stated by Fawn Weaver, "The greatest marriages are built on teamwork, mutual respect, healthy dose of admiration and a never-ending portion of love and grace". A point to dwell on is that if marriage did not have its share of benefits, it would not be one of the oldest and most common institutions in the world.

Chapter 7.

Seven Secrets to Make a Decision

Personally I believe this chapter to be certainly one of the most important parts of this book. This is where you will forge a concrete opinion, if you are or not ready to get married or perhaps with the right person.

Deciding whether or not to marry is one of the toughest decisions for most people. Is that person the right match for me? Will our marriage work? What sacrifice will I have to do for our marital life? Am I doing the right thing? Is this marriage a rebound of my previous one, or do I repeat the same mistake? These are only some of the countless questions that are running through the mind of someone who has to make this decision.

Marriage, as explained in the previous chapters of this book, is a very serious and sensitive matter; it must not be taken lightly. You cannot simply marry another person and break the commitment the next day over an insignificant fight. This is not how this institution should be perceived or exercised anyway. Its sanctity must be comprehended and respected fully by a person before they choose to spend their entire life with another individual.

This is precisely why you must make up your mind about marriage after a considerable amount of thinking, and **only when you are in a sane and sensible state of mind**. Deciding to marry quickly or when you're emotionally unstable is nothing but foolish. To find out whether or not it is the time to settle on marriage and take this undoubtedly huge step in your life, there are a few things that you must understand. These things will also work as secrets to help you decide whether or not marriage is suitable for you at this very point of life.

Love

Ask yourself this simple question before saying, "I do" to the person whom you're considering marrying.

"Why do I love him or her?" The answer to this question lies in the feelings you have for that person. It is very important to find a very decent amount of answers to this question. As simple and maybe stupid as it sound, at first answers will probably going through your mind very easily but the deeper you will go the more difficult it is going to be, and this is where you will find one on the first answers regarding your final decision.

Possibly, you are not completely sure where your relationship stands. Do you have a solid carrying relationship or perhaps just a passion? In a passion case, then you are most likely to feel a head-over-heels type of love with that person all the time. You vision going to be blinded. Feeling we all had one day and of course denied is often at the start of a new relationship were you sit on your own little could and everything is perfect. If you are not completely sure regarding the nature of your relationship than do the same previous step but on the defect side this time, and if you don't find any or very little, well you know where you stand. If that's the case, then it is a clue that your relationship hasn't reached the maturity for marriage yet, and you may need to give up the idea of getting married at least at the moment.

On the contrary, a solid carrying love is entirely different than passion. You see the person as they truly are, with their quality and fault. Been aware and conscious of them will make you go even deeper and completely fulfill your marriage.

Finding the reason is important as it helps you stick to your partner and remain calm when things become tensile in a marriage. You think of the reason why you said yes in the first place and you begin feeling the same way about your spouse once more. My wife and I have gone through lots of fights of course since we have been together, sometimes silent one, sometimes more expressive, but the one thing that has kept us together is our carrying love for each other and the reasons why we were together at the first place.

I asked myself this exact question several times before coming to the decision and I recommend for you to do the same.

Experience

Do you consider having enough relationship experience to judge if the other person is right for you?

Would you not agree with me that before buying a hefty commodity like a house, investing in new car you intent to keep for long time, you would consider looking at it, in every possible angle and go for a long spin before signing the papers. Now how could you tell if what you are about to buy is the best suited for you? Like pretty much everything, the best way to have a concrete opinion about something is to gain experience or get advice from someone who got some. Otherwise how can you tell if this is right for what you need or aspire? My example is not the most romantic but it is very effective and I am pretty sure many of you have been in this case without even realizing it. Earlier I was talking about experience and cars. A couple of years back, I remember having a serious discussion with one of my friends who was confused and loss regarding our relationship as his partner at the time just proposed. Of course she loved him, she has been with him since they graduate and so did say yes almost straightaway, probably even feeling pressured as he proposed in public. She was happy, well in appearance because I could feel in her something was wrong. We were in our living room and sat on her old sofa to have a discussion about it. After quickly explaining to me, her confusion, doubts, I came up with this idea for her to make up her mind.

I asked her:

_"So think about how long have you been driving now? Nine, almost ten years?

_"Well, yes"

_ "And how many cars did you have since you pass your test?"

_ "I think five, why"

_ "Right, now can you remember your first car?"

_ "Of course, it was great" She says smiling"

_ "You know, I remember mine too, it was a small red car, diesel, and with manual windows where you could only open one door and very very slow …

But I thought it was amazing at the time, but when I look at it now, well, it wasn't very good. Was it the same for you?"

_ "Yes indeed you are right, it was fun but not that good!"

_ "And could you remember what was your first though when you bought you second car? You probably thought about all the negative points from your previous one and probably came to a decision where you didn't want it in your second one! And I'm sure you've done the same thing for the one after that, until the one that you drive today, no?"

_ "Yes of course"

_ " So, you will agree with me, the thing that you were doing unconsciously is simply gaining experiences based on your previous feedback acquire along the way. Now relationship has a very similar pattern where experience is vital. So how many boyfriend or relationship have you been in before to decide if this one is the ONE?"

_ "Aah you know, just him"

_ "Now answer my question honestly, having just him as feedback do you consider yourself having enough experience and be in strong position to commit yourself for life with him?"

_ "Mmmmhh, eehh, mmmhh ...."

She was looking up, and her face was expressing the discomfort of our thoughts. She knew now undoubtedly the answer regarding her fiancée and what will have to happen next. I also believed this is why she was feeling confused before we talked, simply because she knew but just didn't want to admit it to herself, possibly as well feeling pressured from friends and relatives.

So, how many feedbacks do you have? And is that enough? I'm absolutely not saying you need to go around and jump on any male or female to obtain experiences. What I'm trying to explain which I'm sure you all understand is, if you are like my friends and just have been in relationship with one single person and are about to get engage for life with them, as previously discuss the odds and statistic are clearly against you.

Gaining experience along the way undeniably will help you to decide what is the most suited for yourself, until I'm sure one day feeling confident, you decide to take the leap. Unfortunately too often people make up their mind built on assumption or simply based on one single experience, waking up one day asking themselves if they are in the right bed? For me it is simply gambling, and don't be one of them.

Future

Another thing you need to be sure about is whether or not you see a future with your partner.

When you visualize your future, is your partner in it with you or are you alone?

Or perhaps do you see yourself with someone else? Think about this clearly. What would be your life with him or her in 10, 15, 20 years or more? Is your partner the most suited to fulfill you needs? This should help you to get decided, has you need to tap into your unconscious, to be able to project yourself and understand whether or not you are ready to marry your partner.

At the time you do this exercise, it is very important to not get confused with the prospect of fear of loss, especially when it's someone that you cherish. If you do that instead of visualizing a happy future projection with your partner, you will use a totally different emotion, which is not love but fear. It is an extremely powerful emotion, but this is not the emotion you want to use to decide on getting married. Do not get clouded between those two as they could feel sometimes very similar on that matter.

Also, when you think of your future, think about one more thing: your core values.

Marrying someone does not mean you have to let go of your habits, likes or dislikes. Although it is certainly not about dismissing your habits, it does demand you to align or compromise your values and beliefs with your spouse. You and your spouse should be on the same page on various important issues like family, residence, children and occupations. If your core values are parallel, it will become quite simple and convenient for both of you to live together peacefully.

If you cannot imagine yourself with your partner, for reasons like, of who they are or how they are and if you picture yourself realistically with someone else, then yes you are definitely not ready get married. Maybe you actually need to move on with your relationship.

On the other hand, if for instance you manage to see you and your better half holding hands smiling to each other, happily walking on a beach on a beautiful sunny day while looking after your grandkids, then you are one step closer to your final decision.

Careers

You need to ask this question. Are your careers compatible?

Do analyze your career and the one of your partner's when making up your mind about marriage. Why this is so important? There are some many different jobs over there and some of them are more compatible than some other. For instance, if you are a farmer and your partner cannot stand to live outside a city. Maybe you are a working in the medical field doing insane hours, but your partner is doing a nine to five Monday to Friday and does not understand why you don't give up your job for a more "normal" life. Or you are working in catering industry and you are completely devoted to your career to be the best, working nights and weekend, where your partner is actually at home resting or perhaps going out with friends. Or your partner is in the army and goes on tour for months without you not knowing really what is he/she doing, adding on the pressure where life-threatening situations are common.

These are only few of the examples of relationship issues you could face because of different career paths. I think career disassociation is probably one of the most difficult reasons to approach when choosing to getting married, as a lot of us do not know exactly where and how we will work in the future.

In general, we all know before we start a relationship what the other does but we sometimes do not fully understand it, and what consequences this type of occupation will have on the relationship.

A lot of times, unfortunately in the long run it is difficult to realize what impact two opposite careers will really have on us as couple. One thing is sure, is that slowly but surely if only one of the person in the relationship is completely devoted to his or her job, and neglects conjugal duties, or does not give enough attention to the other, then they slightly and unconsciously begin sliding apart from each other. This is mostly realized years later because they haven't really shared experiences and enough time together that they have now nothing at all in common other than just living in the same house and unfortunately having kid together.

It is extremely difficult, near impossible to anticipate what will be your or your partner's career for the next ten, twenty or more years, but the things you need to keep in mind despite whatever happens around you, is to stay close and be mentally connected together.

Answering this question is rather hard especially if you are at a relatively young age, but becomes much easier if you are slightly more mature.

Trust

Is their trust between us? This is an answer only your heart can give.

Another extremely important point you need to know before deciding to marry your partner is whether or not, both of you trust each other. Trust will be one of the most valuable assets you marriage will have, and no stable marriage can be built without trust. Ask yourself whether or not you have complete faith in them and have the confidence that they won't betray you and will always remain sincere.

Part of the trust you have in each other is based on reliability. It is fundamental for both counterparts to be reliable. As you will grow together, life will bring you many challenges that you will have to face together and will need to rely on each other to successfully overcome those problems. You also need to know, if your partner places all their trust in you too. Trust in a relationship cannot exist if it comes from just one direction. It has to work on both ways; both of you need to depend on each other and have faith that you two will stay committed to one another.

Trusting your partner doesn't completely mean that you have faith that they won't betray you. It means you know if they will be by your side when you fall sick, or go bankrupt, or meet an accident, suffer from a deadly disease, find out that you are infertile, or face any other hardship that is difficult to bear alone. If your answer is a 'no' to anyone these things, or perhaps you are not convince on one of them, than think twice and reassure trust is there before to say "yes" to that person.

Nanette Newman once said, "A good marriage is at least 80 percent good luck in finding the right person at the right time. The rest is trust."

This beautiful quote shows that once you find your perfect match, the only way you can take that relationship forward and convert it into marriage is by building trust in one another and maintaining it.

Trust is something could who takes years to build and just second to destroy. We all know deep down in our heart if we are with a loyal and trustworthy person. Most of the times, it is just a matter of being honest with ourselves. So be honest…

Sacrifices

How many of us have already made sacrifices for a relationship? Big or small, I can say with confidence that all of us at some point ended up by choosing something different than we would of, if we were single. And you probably did feel as well, you were the only one in the relationship to do all the concession! Marriage cannot work this way and this is why you need to be able to answer the following question.

What sacrifice would he or she be ready to do for our relationship?

Marriage is certainly all about making sacrifices and compromises. Every working relationship is based on that. I'm sure you are aware about what you personally would let go for your partner or the wellness of your relation. But the real question is, do you know what would he or she would let go of to stay with you and for ensuring your happiness? A person who is hundred percent committed to his relationship will be ready to do anything to maintain it successful. On the opposite, the facts are relatively clear if your partner always feels reticent regarding any concession, it means you are not important enough and believe me you do not want to start a marriage on that basis.

Concession can be in the form of small things like choosing the restaurant, or deciding which movie you are going to watch tonight. Sometimes it also can be a life-changing decision such as moving to another country or state, leaving relatives and friends and the comfort of a beautiful house and everything that you own. Life changing sacrifices can only be done within the prospect, (if it is not the case already) of long-term relationship from both partners.

When that happens there is no need to remind constantly your partner of all the sacrifice that you've done for them, but it is important to ensure he or she knows what you have done in measure for them to fully appreciate your commitment.

Although doing concession may be inevitable, when the time comes, it's not always easy. Sacrifice is always the source of major conflict in relationship.

Being aware of your partner's commitment to the relationship can be discovered by simply finding what would they be ready to lose to stay with you. It is also of sense, for you to be ready to do the same thing and sharing your part of the pain when the time comes to return the favor.

Knowing the degree of commitment from you partner will I'm sure help you to decide if he is the right person for you and what you desire.

Gut Feeling

After reading the previous section of this chapter, some of you might probably think, you will never get married because the entire universe need to be aligned with the stars for it to happen.

Though this point is mentioned in the end, but it is nonetheless extremely important. You need to find out your gut feeling. What does your gut say about marrying your partner? Is your sixth sense speaking to you positively or negatively when you think of marriage with your partner? What sort of emotions do you experience when you plan to get married?

There is no exact science regarding marriage and love. If you get positive answers from the six previous questions, but your gut feeling is not there, well don't go for it, or at least not yet. But on the opposite, if you have some doubt about certain answers, from some of the question, but your gut feeling is strongly telling you that he is the one, then you know what you need to do. Jump in!

Your overall feeling is what matter the most but whatever happen do not rust it, many times giving it a bit more thought and it will unconsciously guide you towards a decision. Think of all these questions and your answer several times prior finalizing your decision, but remember there is absolutely no right or wrong choice in all cases, **only feedback to gain experience.**

Chapter 8.

What Will Change
If We Say Yes?

Marrying someone certainly changes your life completely. For some people, only a few aspects of their life change. For instance, if you are mature and have been in a relationship with the same person for ten, fifteen years in which marriage will just be a financial advantage, then your life might not change too much or either at all. While for others, with only few months or years it could feel like an enormous difference between their life as an individual in relationship and their life as married.

Take a look at some of the significant modifications that will take place in your life once you say "I do" to your partner's.

How You Take Your Decisions

One of the biggest changes that you experience after tying the knot is how you make important decisions in life. Whenever you are expected to make a decision, you have to think it from two perspectives: what you find best and what your spouse thinks is best.

This often creates problems for a lot of couples, especially those who aren't used to considering others' opinions during significant decisions. All the things that related to "me" now change to "we". While settling your mind on something, you should not think of what "I want", rather you should focus more on what "we would like".

Therefore, you need to prepare yourself for becoming more open minded and welcoming ideas of making decisions together as a couple. Decisions like where you two both would enjoy living, how you will juggle your professional and personal lives, when you want children and how you would like to raise your kids. All those questions will come as a couple and must be taken after you both reach a consensus.

You Have to Compromise

When you are single, you do whatever you think is best for you and if you don't feel comfortable doing an activity or taking a certain decision, you have the liberty of giving up that idea on the whole or simply changes as you wish. This attitude obviously needs to change once you get married.

Marriage as much as been in a relationship, requires both you, and your spouse, to make many important compromises. You and your spouse cannot do things in the same manner to when you were having separate lives; now you two live together and there will come several situations where one of you won't be comfortable and would like things to change a little or a lot. In such situations, you will have to compromise.

Hence, you two need to be prepared for cooperating with each other and making little to big compromises for the sake of one another. Remember the more you will cooperate, the more your spouse will respect, love and cherish you. However, it is important that you should not be the only one to compromise every time. Remember, compromise is good, and equal compromise is better!

If only one of the spouses is cooperating with the other and making all the sacrifices, then this will place a lot of weight on the one who lets go of everything, resulting sooner or later in arguments, and sometimes even worse, divorce at some point. Therefore, both of you should know the importance of meeting halfway on a situation and should make concessions for each other.

Priorities Change

Your priorities and preferences in life will also change once you get married. Tension could arise when couples are facing friendships outside of their relationship. In a lot of cases, especially men, seem to have a bit more difficulties to let go of the time they used to spend watching or playing football, basketball games, or in even finishing late at night in bars and pubs reshaping the world with mates. Those situations often appear in the beginning of a marriage where a transition has to be made. Many conflicts emerge from them leading to tension in the couple sometimes supported by friends who want you to act as if you were still single.

Understanding and accepting each other's differences is the key to nurturing the friendship within your own relationship and also developing a new one. Maintaining your friendships and interacting with other, could look like juggling while you try to empower your marriage. On the flip side, you may find that you don't have much in common anymore with old friends who spent life as a single person with you.

Meanwhile, it is essential for both spouses to maintain quality time with their friends as it could sometimes help release tensions outside the marital home, but it is also fundamental to dedicate most of your time outside work to your new family.

Your priorities will change even more when you become parents. Then, you would always put your children first and then think about yourself and your spouse. Your number one concern would always be the welfare of your children: their health, their clothes, their education, their happiness and everything else pertinent to them would always be your precedence.

You need to understand that things won't remain once you get married, hence it is better to know what to expect.

Caring for Two Families

It is rightfully said that marriage isn't just union of two people, rather it is a merger of two families. When you get married, you don't only have to worry about your family, but also the family of your spouse.

When you get your married, you expect your spouse to be caring towards your family and it is natural that your spouse will expect the same from you. Your spouse's family would anticipate you to visit or call them on important occasions such as birthdays, Christmas, Easter and Thanksgiving. Similarly, your family would be looking forward to respect, affection and compassion from your spouse.

Therefore, when you decide to say yes, you need to be all set to welcome another family with open arms and shower your love on them as well. Your spouse-to-be must be willing to do the same for your family, so everything stays in balance and you both live a happy married life.

Your Name Changes

Though a lot of married women do not change their surname, there is a population that does modify their name, but laws and regulation will completely vary from one country to another. When you agree to marry your partner, you need to prepare yourself for this change as well.

According to an estimate by the Huffington Post, about eight percent women in America will retain their surnames after getting married. During the 1990s, this number was much higher; it was around 23 percent. Some expect the modernized world to have a different effect on women with the passage of time, but the statistics above are quite opposite to that assumption.

A poll conducted by Huffington Post Weddings in partnership with YouGov gathered the views of a thousand adults in the U.S. regarding whether or not women should change their name on getting married. Over 60 percent of the participants polled that women must take the last name of their husband after marriage. Less than 50 percent of the participants said that the husband should take the last name of his wife.

As a large number of people believe it is better for a wife to take her better half's last name, then it is likely that your spouse will expect the same from you. It is better to communicate your feelings about the name with your spouse if you're not ready for it and want to continue carrying your father's name. However, if you do want to bring that modification to your name, you should gather sufficient information on this subject.

You Argue Differently

Once you turn from single to married, you won't be fighting in the same manner as when they were just your partners. Marriage does bring a huge change to the way you argue with another. This is mainly because of the relationship situation.

Fights between married couples often last for a longer period than those taking place between unmarried couples. When you aren't married, you always have the option of breaking up, saying "THANK YOU" and parting ways. Getting out of a marriage is a lot harder than a relationship or cohabitation. As explained in the previous chapters, marriage is a serious institution with legal implication that cannot be interrupted as easily as people could think. In many times it involves financial retribution and all other sorts of issues, for instance you also need to take in consideration the impact that it would have if there are any young children involved. This is why married couples really need to think a twice before splitting up or perhaps even better, before say "I do".

You'll Address Your Spouse Differently

Another change you will experience on starting your marital life is the way you and your spouse will address one another. While talking to someone, you are most like to address him as "my husband" or her as "my wife". This might seem like an insignificant change right now but once you become married, these words will surely feel very weighty. It takes a few attempts and sometimes at the beginning could sound odd, but I am sure that introducing your other half will make you proud.

This is an important part of your relationship evolving that demands you to act accordingly as well. Now, don't fret because things won't become terrible when you marry. If you truly love your partner and are ready to take a big leap in your life, then these words will seem nothing, but pleasant to you. On the contrary, if it is not the case, then it means you aren't completely ready yet.

You Feel More Secure

The moment you become married, you would feel a new sense of safety. This feeling of security provides you with the comfort that you will always have someone close to you on whom you can depend on without thinking twice.

This feeling will also raise the expectations you have from your other half. You will want him or her to be by your side whenever you times are tough and to provide you with warmth and unconditional affection. Your spouse will anticipate the same from you. You both need to support, nurture and love each other no matter what.

No doubt this feeling is beautiful, but it also demands you to be devoted towards your spouse at all time, and act as he or she could reach your support whenever they need to.

Chapter 9.

Final Thoughts

The beginnings of marriage or its introduction to the human race is mentioned in numerous, stories, legends and religious scriptures across the world, its importance in shaping the structure of family as we know it. Religion and culture give marriage a sanctity that makes it a sacred act protected by scripture, supported by society, and enforced by the law. Though these stories vary from culture to culture, the key aspects of marriage remain similar. It gives importance to a legal binding between a man and a woman and encourages them to build a home where they will bear and raise children. This philosophy, though simplistic in its fundamental purpose, was meant to aid the development of humans and society in an organized and favorable method.

Marriage and wedding practices vary according to regional culture and religion. Age, sexual orientation and religion are just three of the multiple other factors that may dictate the structure of a marriage. For example, in Muslim countries a man is allowed up to four wives, so the concept of polygamy is very different from that in most western countries. Similarly, while it is becoming increasingly possible for same-sex couples to legally wed in the developed world, in the developing world this is not usually the case or even worse has been reprimanded.

Tradition and symbolism heavily dictate marriage and wedding rituals in all societies. In Christianity, the rings worn by a husband and wife symbolize that they are married whereas in Hinduism a woman wears red vermillion on her forehead to symbolize that she is betrothed.

Humans mark their lives with the milestones that they reach; rites of passage are observed and key moments celebrated. Whether it is a teenager in the U.S. attending graduation or a tribal boy in Africa taking part in a customary rite of passage, events are perceived importantly in human progression. Likewise, many traditionalists and some modern theorists argue that marriage is a milestone event that can shape a person's life. With this theory in mind, marriage would mean that a person has graduated from one phase in their life to the next. For example, where they were first responsible for only themselves, they now have progressed onto having responsibility in someone else's life as well.

The added responsibility of marriage may not suit those who chose to remain unmarried to avoid the restrictions that it brings. Others who are in successful relationships may choose to avoid marriage simply because of the label it carries. Sometimes a choice based on their previous personal or relatives experiences, perhaps purely because they don't want to be placed in this category.

While it may be true that relationships exist outside marriage as well, many individuals and let's be honest in general more women than men, consider marriage to be a crucial or even natural next step in the development of a relationship. Is it strange then that so many same-sex couples are passionately fighting for their right to marry, regardless of already being together in a union of sorts?

Many modern couples choose not to marry and claim that it is not a requirement, or even go as far as announcing that marriage may prove to actually be detrimental to their relationship. They quote numerous couples who were happy together for years and became estranged shortly after getting married. Some argue that their relationship or love does not need a legal document to bind it.

In most cultures around the world, a successful life is marked stereotypically with a home, spouse, children and a job. Whereas the home and job are required to meet a physical need, the spouse provides emotional support and companionship, and children continue your bloodline.

We are socialized from a very young age to want to accomplish those things that will deem us as successful. The Harvard Grant study mentored by George Vaillant, a Harvard psychiatrist was conducted between 1972 to 2004 and found that love was the most important factor needed in living a fulfilling happy life. It is no surprise, then, that striving to achieve an emotional and physical bond with others is a considered basic human nature.

However, the notion of marriage being of the ultimate importance in human life is argued upon greatly. In a 2010 Pew Research Survey conducted amongst the American public, results showed that "about half or more think there is no difference between being married or single in the ease of having a fulfilling sex life, being financially secure, finding happiness, getting ahead in a career or having social status". Technically, none of these factors are guaranteed in a marriage.

Those wishing to marry have to first identify and pursue a partner who they wish to wed. That partner has to agree to fulfill the requirements of the marriage. For example, if the purpose of the marriage is to provide financial support or to bear children, those factors become crucial in choosing a spouse. The partner should also be committed to the life choices they decide on as a couple. For instance, whether they actually want to have children or live in a certain place.

What is very important is to consider is the legal implications of entering into a marriage contract. Marriage laws worldwide dictate a variety of factors, such as the legal rights of spouses. Financial implications like taxes and inheritance, with regard to legal partners, are also determined by law. Finally, legal repercussions exist for those wanting to separate from their spouses or dissolve their marriage. In some countries such as the Philippines and in the Christian Catholic religion, one is not allowed to terminate their marriage. Not having the option of a life-long binding may prove highly dissuading, if not at least daunting, to members of such communities.

Overall, however, with the rising number of divorces (almost 50% of marriage) and increasing number of people deciding against marriage, many governments have amended laws and legislation to be pro-marriage. Tax holidays for couples are one such example. These laws have also been designed to make divorce increasingly difficult and costly. As marriage is a legally binding contract, legal consent is needed to dissolve one. And yet we easily could see around us divorce becoming as much as marriage, just another normal step in our adult life.

Each modern individual wanting a wedding asks themselves whether it's the right step to take in view of what they want from their life. Simply put many marry for happiness. Whether it's the love of a spouse, the warmth of a companion or the satisfaction of children, marriage is more often than not seen as a means to an end. It is here that we find the biggest opposition. Many theorists claim that the increasing numbers of studies prove that marriage affects a relationship, most often in a negative manner. These theorists also lay claim to the fact that love and companionship, along with other factors that induce happiness and the feeling of fulfillment, can be achieved without the legal binding and subsequent drawbacks of marriage. According to the Huffington Post, "Global surveys have found that cultural norms and expectations are what determine our self-esteem, even if we claim we're above the pressure... this dual mentality can get tricky. The (obvious) truth is that marriage -- or even long-term couple-hood -- won't make everyone happier."

The result is that many modern day couples are choosing not to get married. Sometimes a couple may live together, build a home, raise children, and live in what is considered the most traditional of fashion, but may not choose to legalize their relationship with a contract.

Many people believe that marriage also has numerous benefits, both emotional and physical, that cannot be found in those that choose not to indulge in it. Married people are most likely to admit that the act has changed their relationship but many will also tell you that it's for the better. "It's not marriage that makes you happy, it's a happy marriage that makes you happy," Daniel Gilbert, a researcher at Harvard, once said. Married people are happier than unmarried ones, perhaps because the single best predictor of human happiness is the quality of social relationships. "The highest happiness on earth is the happiness of marriage" William Lyon Phelps.

The truth is that marriage, like most important things, has its advantages and its disadvantages. Many therapists argue that it is often not the marriage the problems, but the individuals whose personal problems and behavior begin to reflect on their marriages, and they are obviously true. Therefore, it is essential that individuals entering into wedlock or not observe themselves and their partner to make themselves fit for the challenges marriage involves. It is also crucial, for both partners to do their homework to eradicate as much as possible any personal doubt, especially before doing any decisive life commitment.

Following those 7 Steps describe earlier in the book, will I hope, guide you through this extremely difficult process of decision making which will certainly end up confirming or disapproving what could be most undoubtedly one of the biggest decision of your entire life.

Useful Links and Resources

Advice and Benefits

1. www.drphil.com

Dr. Phil McGraw is a celebrity in mainstream mental health and the media world. Launched in 2002, his website is a causal and inviting approach to mental health issues, which include emotional and behavioral problems faced by married couples. Here, individuals and couples can study the root cause behind their respective problems and learn about how they can bring about change.

2. www.marriagehelper.com

Joe Beam is a celebrity self-help expert and experienced marriage counselor. His seminars and workshops are based on a modernistic approach to marriage, catering to new–age couples with problems and issues current to the times. He is known to have helped hundreds of troubled couples. His website houses numerous articles and activities by him, as well as information regarding his live seminars.

3. http://loveandlifetoolbox.com/

The Toolbox is a comprehensive website authored by a known educationalist in the field of marriage counseling, Lisa Brookes Kift. The website has received much acclaim due to the vast amount of knowledge and information it provides couples in recognizing and dealing with marital issues. With a focus on mental and emotional health and its effect on relationships, the website empowers individuals to work on themselves and their marriage.

Laws around the World

1. http://www.freedomtomarry.org/landscape/entry/c/international

A project of civil rights attorney, Evan Wolfson, Freedom to Marry works at aiding and striving toward marriage equality in the United States and rest of the world. The website provides comprehensive information regarding laws, petitions, and legal requirements to LGBTQ couples. It also works as an educational forum for those wishing to learn about same-sex marriage policies and is updated regularly with related news from around the world.

2. http://family.findlaw.com/

Family Law is an easy-to-use legal information website authored by a group of lawyers with extensive experience on family and marriage-related laws. It informs the visitor as to the prevailing laws and in what circumstances they would need to hire a professional counselor. The site is extremely helpful to those couples dealing with issues like immigration, child custody, inheritance and divorce.

3. http://family.findlaw.com/marriage/marriage-license-requirements.html

Find Law is a website that caters to those looking for legal information, as well as hiring legal counsel. The website has information pertaining to marriage laws and requirements in the United States and a general overview of what may be legal in other countries around the world. It is particularly helpful for couples wishing to get married as it provides an accurate timeline to how long procedures such as acquiring a marriage license will take.

Online Counselors

1. www.marriageadvice.com

Marriage Advice is a site that has numerous contributors to it. This includes advice and testimonials from counselors, psychiatrists, lawyers and married couples, all of who can provide an in-depth and comprehensive view into the dynamics of coupling and matrimony.

2. www.marriagemax.com

Mort Fertel, the force behind MarriageMax is a renowned psychiatrist and a famed couple's counselor. He runs programs such as the Marriage Fitness Tele-Boot Camp and is the creator of the Marriage Fitness Audio Learning System and the Marriage Fitness Home-Flex. His hands-on approach to dealing with marital issues is revolutionary and has shown commendable results in thousands of couples all over the world.

3. http://thecoupleconnection.net/

The Couples Connect is a UK-based site that uses the help of articles, quizzes, a relationship-forum and their listening room to empower couples to address their own problems. Counselors are available for advice, but the general theme of the website is directed towards self-help. This website may be a good option for those who shy from seeking external help or want to take matters into their own hands.

Articles by Married People

1. www.projecthappilyeverafter.com

Alisa Bowman started the website Project Happily Ever After to document her own journey through the turmoil and eventual triumph of her marriage. She now acts as a self-help guru, providing genuine and heartfelt advice to couples in need. The site hosts Bowman's blog posts and a free e-book, along with content from various other resources. The site may be refreshing for those who wish to consult someone more like themselves, as opposed to seeking professional assistance.

2. http://www.huffingtonpost.com/2014/09/02/loverly-marriage-advice_n_5733484.html

The article titled 19 Solid Pieces of Marriage Advice from Wedding Bloggers is a light and humorous piece with a definite feel-good factor. The advice coming from people who in a way specialize in marriage – but not really the problems associated with it – offers heartfelt, easily understandable words of wisdom to those wishing to embark on this journey or to those who are already a part of it.

3. http://marriagegems.com/

Lori Lowe runs a highly researched blog called Marriage Gems. It hosts a variety of interviews, blog posts and articles about the topics related to marriage. Contributors to the site range from counselors, therapists, love gurus, and even the novice spouse. The layout of the site is friendly and easy to navigate and the content is bound to have something of interest for everyone.

Conclusion

The Greek philosopher Heraclitus once said that nothing in this world remains constant, except for change. Marriage is a milestone for most people and it is marked by significant change. This change is neither good nor bad, but is relative to what one makes of it or eventually what shape and direction our lives take because of it. Some cherish the change and what it brings in their lives, others resent it for what it took away from them. Marriage is an ancient phenomenon introduced through both religion and culture to mark a step forward in the relationship and subsequently life of a man and a woman.

Whilst attempting to exactly define marriage, Anthropologists have faced numerous challenges when attempting to word a phenomenon that is so common and yet so varied in nature. As stated by Evan Gerstmann, "The definitions of marriage have careened from one extreme to another and everywhere in between."

Marriage as an institution made up of numerous elements. Factors such as legislation, culture, financial dependency and wider society are all players in shaping marriage. These, along with numerous others, determine how two individuals are going to get married and how they're going to live their marriage. With the influence of so many elements, the biggest factor that shapes a marriage remains the individuals that partake in it. Though a major part of marriage is objective in nature, such as its legal and financial implications, other parts like emotional wellbeing, physical intimacy, and loyalty are fairly subjective and can be customized by the married couple, thus deeming it relatively flexible and adaptable in nature.

Though the fundamental principle of marriage remains similar throughout the world, it is primarily an official binding that unites two individuals; marriage itself may have a different implication for different people. In different societies throughout the world, marriage hold varying consequences for the couple involved. In eastern countries, for example, marriages take place between younger members of society as opposed to the west, where the age bracket of those getting married is increasingly on the rise. Responsibility and requirements also differ in regions. In South Asian countries, it is usually the men who are required to financially support their female spouse and subsequently their children. This practice is fading in the west; an increasing percentage of women enter the workforce every year. Men in such countries are under no legal obligation to solely provide for their family, and the decision to do so is taken entirely by the married couple.

Rising divorce rates throughout the world and strict legislation make the annulment of marriage relatively difficult and somewhat complicated. Some countries and religions condone divorce, making it extremely difficult for a spouse to separate from their significant other. These factors act as a warning sign to those who have yet to indulge in matrimony. In any case, experts in the field will advise to never undermine the sanctity of marriage or not give the decision to marry its due diligence.

Many western societies are now openly supportive of families and relationships that fall into traditional definitions. This gives couples the room to decide whether marriage really is what their relationship or their life requires. Many cite love as their main reason for being together and argue that if love exists in the relationship, they don't need financial and legal clauses to bind them. Others, however, want the security of a legal binding before investing time and energy into a relationship.

Despite all the positives and negatives, marriage remains widely popular throughout the world, even in the most liberal and developed of nations. In the U.S., even though marriage is at an all-time statistical low of 51 per cent, in a 2010 Pew Research Centre survey, marriage remained a top priority for those who weren't already married. About 61 per cent of men and women who have never married say they would like to get married, but only 12 per cent say they do not want to marry and 27 per cent are still unsure.

Marriage, as an institution, is generally revered around the world. In the majority of cultures and religions, it marks a progression in one's life; its start is celebrated and its end is mourned. Some argue that men and women are designed to live in pairs. We seek emotional and physical bonds because attaining those make us happy.

What should never influence any person into marriage are elements that may influence an individual or marriage, but are not essential in maintaining it. Factors such as financial dependency and social pressure dictate numerous marriages, especially in the developing world. They, however, do not necessarily make for the happiest ones. In addition, even in the developed world, women especially may need the feel to get married because all their friends are married, or men may feel that being unmarried is not beneficial to their career and comfort. In essence, marriage is a prospect that is meant to be long lasting and its success often entails a lot of commitment, hard work and emotional sensitivity. It is no way a decision to be taken lightly.

Before stepping into the formal contract and emotional bond that is marriage, think sensibly and study your options thoroughly. Marriage may not be for everyone in the world, but it is something that should certainly be considered.

A few final words

You've reached the end of the book, and I wanted to say thank you for reading. It has been a great pleasure to do this first book, in which my main goal has been to help others going through this doubtful time of life. I wanted to share this very personal experience, and the process I been through before deciding.

I truly hope you enjoyed reading this book and found it informative, and most importantly helpful in regards to making your decision or having a better understanding of what to expect if you decide to get married.

Please do not hesitate to contact me if you need any help in your decision, or clarification regarding the 7 secrets.

Remember:

You are where you are today because all the experience you've had in your life, and can only be where you are because of those experiences. Live life as it should be lived.

To the beginning of a journey . . .

DISCLAIMER: This book details the author's personal experiences with and opinions about <u>Reasons to get Married, The ULTIMATE confirmation or disapproval</u>. The author is not licensed as an educational consultant, teacher, psychologist, or psychiatrist.

The author and publisher are providing this book and its contents on an "as is" basis and make no representations or warranties of any kind with respect to this book or its contents. The author and publisher disclaim all such representations and warranties, including for example warranties of merchantability and educational or medical advice for a particular purpose. In addition, the author and publisher do not represent or warrant that the information accessible via this book is accurate, complete or current.

The statements made about products and services have not been evaluated by the U.S. or UK government or any other. Please consult with your own legal or accounting professional regarding the suggestions and recommendations made in this book.

Except as specifically stated in this book, neither the author or publisher, nor any authors, contributors, or other representatives will be liable for damages arising out of or in connection with the use of this book. This is a comprehensive limitation of liability that applies to all damages of any kind, including (without limitation) compensatory; direct, indirect or consequential damages; loss of data, income or profit; loss of or damage to property and claims of third parties.

You understand that this book is not intended as a substitute for consultation with a licensed medical, educational, legal or accounting professional. Before you begin any change in your lifestyle in any way, you will consult a licensed professional to ensure that you are doing what's best for your situation.